Tony Conigliaro is a revolutionary. He is at the forefront of a new energy in cocktail making. His research is exhaustive and his commitment has resulted in some delicious and innovative cocktails.

His inspiration comes from such diverse extremes as movies and perfumes and his knowledge of alcohol history dates back to alchemy itself. He has a great insight into the spirits and the alcohol he uses and the various processes of their creation. This solid foundation of knowledge is the building block for his creativity. His respect and understanding of the produce he uses in his drinks result in delicious, intense flavours as he pushes the rules of classic cocktail-making beyond expectation.

Tony's enthusiasm does not just stop with the drink in the glass. He is concerned with every component, from the presentation, colour, smell, type of receptacle used, to the way in which the ice is frozen and its effects on taste and flavour. By using modern equipment not normally associated with the tools of a cocktail barman, Tony manages to extract the best possible flavours from his marinades and infusions, resulting in a cleaner, sharper quality of cocktail. His commitment to research and development is a breath of fresh air and he has a strong focus on reinventing iconic classics.

With the publication of the recipes in *Drinks*, the skill and enthusiasm that Tony brings to the industry, combined with his pure raw energy, will help the enthusiast to unfold the mysteries surrounding his philosophy and approach to cocktail making – and maybe trigger a few ideas of their own.

HESTON BLUMENTHAL

DRINKS

Tony Conigliaro

EBURY
PRESS

For my mentors Richard 'Dick' Bradsell, Rainer 'ja ja' Becker for believing in me, and my dear friend Audrey 'smell this' Saunders, for all the incredible walks and talks.

And for Ria 'my Lighting Bolt' Soler, well, for being the lighting bolt.

Last but not least, Gemma 'you're driving me mad' Reeves, without whom this book would not be possible.

13 5 7 9 10 8 6 4 2

Published in 2012 by Ebury Press, an imprint of Ebury Publishing
A Random House Group Company
Text © Tony Conigliaro 2012
Photography © Ebury Press 2012

Tony Conigliaro has asserted his right to be identified as the author of this Work in accordance with the Copyright, Designs and Patents Act 1988

The Random House Group Limited Reg. No. 954009

Addresses for companies within the Random House Group can be found at www.randomhouse.co.uk

A CIP catalogue record for this book is available from the British Library

The Random House Group Limited supports The Forest Stewardship Council® (FSC®), the leading international forest certification organisation. Our books carrying the FSC label are printed on FSC® certified paper. FSC is the only forest certification scheme endorsed by the leading environmental organisations, including Greenpeace. Our paper procurement policy can be found at www.randomhouse.co.uk/environment

To buy books by your favourite authors and register for offers visit www.randomhouse.co.uk

Design by Allies Design
Photography by Addie Chinn
Illustrations by Juri Nishi

Printed and bound in China by C & C Offset Printing Co., Ltd
ISBN 9780091948658

Contents

I.
DRINKS

In The Beginning There Was Art

There's a beginning to every story. This story begins in a white box-room
with a sink, a rickety second-hand chair, an easel and a table – the top
of which was piled with bills. It was in this room that I discovered that
supporting yourself *after* art school is as challenging as life *at* art school!
After studying fine art and art history in London, I specialised in painting
and experimented with using aroma in paint. In this sense, I've always been
interested in working in one arena but exchanging ideas with an entirely
different discipline. More from necessity than anything else, I began
working in the bar industry – quite simply I needed to fund my studio
work. The crossover between the two disciplines was truly surprising.
I had no idea of the creativity involved in working with cocktails. The two
passions overlapped and then slowly one overtook the other. And so my love
affair with liquids began.

Although art and cocktails seem to be disparate disciplines, they are both
about appealing to sensory experience. At art school I read a lot about the
philosophy of aesthetics and I asked myself questions all the time: why
does one thing appeal to the senses over another, or appeal to just one of
our senses rather than all? I think that there is real beauty in simplicity, in
functionality. Cocktails are often talked about with a lack of sentimentality,
yet many find it easy to become rapturous over wine. When I began to work
in the bar industry the focus started to shift. I wondered: why is flavour in
liquids beautiful?

And Then There Was Flavour

When we ask questions about flavour, our natural response is to turn to the culinary experience as a frame of reference. I love to cook and I revel in the dining experience. Growing up in a Sicilian family, I've always been surrounded with simple, flavour-packed home cooking. I taste dishes over and over again, comparing similar flavours, using the same ingredients with different variations. One of my favourite dishes to cook at home is wild mushroom risotto. Over the years I've honed the recipe to perfection and this is because the devil really is in the detail. Each element of the risotto is important; it's about using just the right amount of stock, the quality and variety of the mushrooms, and I replace white wine with dry vermouth for a lovely nutty flavour. The enjoyment of the finished dish is dependent upon all these small details working in harmony to achieve the perfect final texture.

In fact, much of what we enjoy about food is centred around texture and chewing, but with liquids the mechanism of how you taste is different. People tend to think that taste is just flavour on the tongue, but in actuality the salty/sweet/sour aspects of flavour are also like touch – a sensation, not just a flavour in themselves. Flavour is only really released when you swallow something. At the back of your palate is the epiglottis, which is open when you breathe; when you swallow it closes so that the liquid doesn't flow down into your airways. When it reopens, it releases a reflux of aroma molecules back into the olfactory chamber – so when you're tasting something, you're really smelling it. Therefore, the majority of taste is smell and this is also why the way in which we enjoy cocktails can have much in common with how we enjoy perfumes as well as food.

For this reason, when it comes to liquids there is little or no distraction of texture, of masticating – no knife, no fork. Alcohol can be a fantastic vehicle for delivering immediate flavour. In this sense we are slaves to the first few seconds of taste and it is in those moments that we'll decide whether or not we like a cocktail; our decision whether we love or loathe a drink is rarely an afterthought – the flavour may keep on developing in our mouth but it wins or loses at that first point. There's a huge challenge in this: to fulfil a person's sensory experience immediately!

Cocktails are a niche market and they employ a nebulous space. They don't sit comfortably in the food category, but because they are ingested rather than inhaled it doesn't feel right to consider them in the same spectrum as perfume either. Part of understanding the beauty in liquid flavour comes from trying to find a language that expresses working with liquids for liquid's sake. One of the first steps in creating your own language is to borrow the terminology and signifiers and when talking about cocktails it makes sense to turn to cocktail historians, perfumers and chefs. Challenging the traditional approach to working with alcohol and the language we use to discuss it is no easy feat. Taking about how booze makes you feel is almost a taboo subject – essentially we are discussing the effects of a drug, so how can this be art – how can this be beautiful? People will drink alcohol whether or not it tastes good; we don't grow up drinking alcoholic drinks – we haven't spent a lifetime drinking in the same way that we have eating. And so we have to educate our palates much later in life. I think however, that there is an inherent sense of artistry in drink because of its frivolity – you don't need to have a Bellini, but it's a damn good feeling when you do.

Studying the Structure

Drinks are by no means universally delicious but there are solid reasons why some just taste better than others. To make a truly delicious cocktail you have to triumph over flavour; manipulate it, have a command over it, and the only way to achieve this is to understand its structure. So I often pull the different components of the cocktail apart, study them separately and then put the cocktail back together in the way that I want it. I've spent years studying the structure of drink in this manner, not just reading and researching, but experimenting, testing a formula and pushing its boundaries. If you sample a Dry Martini in 20 or 30 different ways then you simply have a better insight than you would merely trusting theories and reading recipes. Bartending is a craft.

The passion and dedication that I put into each cocktail can span months, and on occasion, even years. I don't believe in cobbling stuff together. I refine things, test things, make them 100 times over to push the limits until I achieve exactly what I set out to. It's important not simply to accept the first result; there are usually more interesting findings sitting just behind it. I always tinker with the projects that I'm working on, as well as revisiting old projects because there is always a new way of doing things. Every recipe has space to be refreshed, to be renewed, over time. It's true of anything: the more energy you put into something, the better the product.

The linchpin of this approach to drinks is the Drink Factory consultancy, research and development company which I founded in 2005. Now housed in Pink Floyd's old recording studios, the Drink Factory has its own laboratory – the first of its kind in the UK, focusing as it does entirely on alcohol-development and research into liquid flavour. Home to sophisticated lab machinery such as the centrifuge and Rotavapor the lab functions to produce bespoke ingredients and develop new recipes. With clients as diverse as chefs, perfume houses, chocolatiers and soft drinks companies, an ordinary day in the lab can involve thermo-mixing, sous-viding, dehydrating – even stripping bark from trees!

The collection of equipment housed at the laboratory is nothing sort of esoteric but each piece of machinery shares the same goal – to match the level of accuracy and innovation of ideas and flavour combinations that chefs worldwide are able to achieve, but to translate this knowledge from the kitchen to the bar world. It's not being niche, rather it's about reaching for the unimagined, to create new combinations, to appeal to all five senses, as well as the sixth sense – instinct. The equipment in the lab quantifies what I aim to do intuitively. Throughout this book the measurements of ingredients vary from millilitres, grams and microns (1000th of a gram). Although this may seem unusual, it is a deliberate move with a view towards total accuracy at all times. When making individual cocktails I always use a jigger to measure each component to ensure that the drink is made exactly the same each time. The same approach goes for pre-preparing or making ingredients in batch, which often involves measuring in a mixture of grams and millilitres. In this way, cocktails are all about emotional functionality – to make something repeatedly wonderful.

Over the years I have worked at numerous bars including Isola and the Shochu Lounge, all of which were instrumental in developing my approach to drinks. The real turning point for me, however, was in 2009 when I opened my own venue, 69 Colebrooke Row, in Islington, North London. The bar was designed as a 1950s-style Italian Café with film noir touches, whilst retaining a 'living-room' feel to encourage an intimate, friendly atmosphere. The menu at Colebrooke Row is deceptively simple: twelve cocktails with minimal descriptors, three wines and champagnes and just one beer. Without prior knowledge customers have no idea just how much work goes into creating the bespoke ingredients used in their cocktails. I like to keep the science and processes out of the customer's direct experience; bartending isn't simply about the drinks – it's as much about hosting and high levels of service. Those customers who do want to know more tend to ask. I like the idea that the rest will contentedly sip on a Bloody Mary, blissfully unaware that it took two years to perfect each individual component of their drink.

History and Mythology

Technology is an extremely important means of progression. However, it's not the sole focus of my drinks. The world of cocktails is rich in history, and coming from a background in art history I simply extended my learning. However, a lot of cocktail history remains impenetrable and it can be very hard to distinguish the truth from mythology. I think this can be an asset! Whilst recognising that deconstructing cocktail history is part of learning to be analytic and understanding why things work, fantasy and mythology have their merits too, and what I love about this duality is that it can be utilised for the benefit of the cocktail experience. Playing upon mythology means that we can create a refuge or suspension from reality – which is exactly what drinking and bars are about. You go to a bar to get away from the craziness of everyday life. Part of the psychology of drinking is to separate a piece of yourself from the whole. I love the look on a customer's face when I explain exactly how their seemingly simple-looking Bloody Mary actually came together. It's as if you can create a stage and all the flavours and characters have to dance around and play their parts within it. Like telling ghost stories around the campfire, I start the first paragraph of the story and the customer defines the next. They may tell a friend about their experience in the bar and that person subsequently writes the following chapter.

I'm often asked whether I believe that we are living in a second golden age of cocktails. Years ago it was a struggle to find good cocktail books but now there is an abundance of information; the internet is buzzing, alive with blogs and foodie websites, and there are bar shows all over the world. This flow of information is incredible and it stimulates a lot of discourse around cocktails. It's completely different from the first golden age of cocktails because there was so much less out there. If you are lucky enough to talk to people from that era, they trained and they read what was available – cocktail knowledge was far more obtuse.

The cocktail world is indeed changing. In the past 15 to 20 years, the bartending world has evolved and it continues to do so. Bartenders exercise their expertise not just through the medium of what has come before them, but rather they are a generation that wants to put its own mark on drinks. As the industry has grown, it has become more creative. The modern bartender is all about creating his or her own style; just like chefs, particular people for their personal styles of drinks. Attitude to drink is also changing. The way people appreciate food and drink nowadays, especially in the UK, has changed dramatically. It's not simply the bartenders who have worked really hard towards this, but the drinks community as a whole who have pushed the boundaries of what people drink. Customers are more demanding – they know more about drinks and it's important that we feed that enthusiasm.

'Drinks'

The recipes in this book demonstrate the different styles that I have worked in: the simple, difficult and the stuff in between. The first five chapters naturally developed their own characters, and it wasn't until I started to revisit old recipes that they began to evolve into quite distinct areas of interest. I found that the drinks shared a genealogy – an idea was born, then pushed, then pushed further, changing slightly and then being changed again. I would look at the ingredients of a cocktail one way and then this would open up a new line of thinking – a chain reaction – just like my initial involvement in the cocktail industry.

New cocktails are usually born from experimenting with flavour connections and listening to a gut instinct. The recipes in this book are often quite romantic in nature. Yes, they have historical references but they go beyond that. Inspiration can come from many places, not always obviously related to cocktails, and they straddle diverse terrains – from perfume to films, poetry to an image of a landscape. Others were inspired by well-loved regulars at my bars – characters worthy of a book in themselves! These stories imbue a hint of fantasy to otherwise quite technical products. I have to be very thankful for my distractions!

When I said earlier that cocktails occupy a nebulous place, so too does this book. It is not a classic cocktail book, nor is it a bar manual. There are recipes here for the home enthusiast but also for the technician. Some of the recipes are known or have solid references, but here my aim is to demonstrate there can be a new point of interest or perspective – what inspired them, how they came together, how they've changed and why they work. Consider it a guide to liquid flavour...

1.
CLASSICS & SPINS

Introduction

Classics & Spins

There are but a handful of cocktails that become survivors of history; more often than not, cocktail recipes are history's victims. The past few years have seen a revival in sourcing classic cocktail recipes and making them to their exact original specification. This resurgence has helped us to develop a cultural and social understanding of that cocktail's epoch, which can tell us as much about the bartender who was making it as the person who consumed it.

Everything has a genealogy that links it to the past and the classics are important for learning our trade, to understand structure, techniques and how flavours work. However, adhering to a blind belief in classic drinks is to negate the extraordinary hard work of the modern bartender and modern times. Too often we have been guilty of being dismissive of the new and sticking with the security of the classics. This argument was more valid when we bartenders were unsure of ourselves and our trade. But I now believe that the idea is to keep pushing the boundaries and combinations until something sticks – this is how modern classics are born.

For me, one of the most exciting aspects of discovering classic recipes is to modernise them – to find a way to make them work so that they are more accessible or acceptable to the modern palate. As the cocktail enthusiastic David Embury once so poignantly acknowledged, cocktails work around basic structures. But if you start playing with each component – taking one out, putting one in and exchanging it – then that structure starts to waver somewhat. The drink does not have to be clearly defined; you can shift things slightly.

What's new is old and what's old is new. It's how you approach the old that makes it new – how you bring things back to life, otherwise these drinks become lost in cocktail books, hidden away from the general public. Learning and growing, alongside technological advances, have made revisiting traditional, simple cocktail recipes an interesting and unique experience. I really enjoy taking a 200-year-old recipe and applying modern processes, which can result in a slicker, more flavourful and more direct drink. Recipes evolve, as do palates, and consequently we must keep abreast of that evolution.

For me, one of the most exciting aspects of discovering classic recipes is to modernise them – to find a way to make them work so that they are more accessible or acceptable to the modern palate.

During the 15 years that I have been working in the industry, I have made the same classic cocktail in countless different ways. The following chapter showcases my tried-and-tested classic cocktail recipes, a lot of which are the drinks that I most like to consume! The recipes that sit beside them are the 'spins' – the drinks that I went on to create, which were inspired by their predecessors but took their flavour profile and waltzed them off into a new direction.

Buck's Fizz

1. Pour the juice into a cocktail tin and follow with the champagne.

2. Stir slowly with a bar spoon before pouring into a champagne flute.

Clementine Buck's Fizz [2007]

This version of the Buck's Fizz uses freshly pressed organic clementine juice for its sweet, floral taste, which complements the acidity of the orange juice. However, it is using a homogeniser that really sets this drink apart from other Buck's Fizz. The oils from the zest stretch the citrus flavour further by providing a slight bitterness – a flavour that usually reaches the palate last, as bitter chemicals are bigger and take longer to get inside the mouth. The job of our saliva is to break down the size of particles in order to taste them, but a homogeniser breaks down all the filaments and walls of the zest for us, dividing them into small particles. This makes the taste process more immediate and fulfilling.

Getting the balance right in this drink took a while because the acidity levels of the fruit must work in harmony with those of the champagne. This Buck's Fizz is a perfect example of how simple drinks often require only small adjustments to transform them into something truly outstanding.

1. Pour the juice mix into a cocktail tin and follow with the champagne.

2. Stir slowly with a bar spoon before pouring into a champagne flute or coupette.

INGREDIENTS
— 25ml homogenised orange and clementine juice (page 163)
— 100ml champagne

Pink Grapefruit Buck's Fizz ²⁰¹⁰

1. Pour the juice into a cocktail tin and follow with the champagne.

2. Stir slowly with a bar spoon before pouring into a champagne flute or coupette.

INGREDIENTS
— 25ml homogenised
  pink grapefruit juice
  (page 163)
— 100ml champagne

Clementine Buck's Fizz

Death in Venice

Sbagliato

1. Build the Campari and vermouth in a rocks glass over cubed ice. Stir and top with the Prosecco.

2. Stir again and garnish with a slice of orange.

INGREDIENTS

— 25ml Campari
— 25ml sweet vermouth
— 75ml Prosecco
— Orange slice, to garnish

Death in Venice ²⁰¹⁰

I have always liked Italy's concept of the *aperitivo* hour. A stopgap between lunch and late dinner, enjoying an aperitif-style drink – whether it be a Negroni, Sbagliato or Spritz – becomes a real social event and a civilised way to unwind from work and begin the evening. My business partner, Camille, loves Campari, Spritzers and Venice. This drink, as well as being an ode to the aperitif, is my ode to her and her liquid loves.

The Sbagliato was the launch pad for this drink, but I was after a lighter cocktail that could mirror its complexities whilst being as refreshing as a Spritz. The result was a cocktail that carefully pivots on a complex interplay between Campari, with its heavily bitter orange flavour, zesty dry grapefruit bitters and Prosecco. A small orange twist completes the layering of multidimensional touches that harmonise bitterness, dryness and citrus for a fresh and lively finish. Served in a champagne flute, this drink packs in far more flavour than just an ordinary Spritz.

1. Pour the Campari into a champagne flute.

2. Add three dashes of homemade grapefruit bitters and top with the Prosecco.

3. Stir gently. Finish with a small twist of orange.

INGREDIENTS

— 15ml Campari
— 3 dashes of homemade grapefruit bitters (page 192)
— 125ml Prosecco
— Orange twist (page 221), to finish

White Gin Fizz

Silver Gin Fizz

1. Combine the gin, lemon juice, sugar syrup and egg white in a cocktail tin.

2. Dry-shake and shake again over cubed ice. Strain into a highball glass with one cube of ice in it, top with soda water and gently stir.

INGREDIENTS
— 35ml gin
— 20ml fresh lemon juice
— 15ml sugar syrup
— 20ml egg white
— Soda water, to top

White Gin Fizz ²⁰⁰⁰

I find the classic Silver Gin Fizz, which uses egg white, to be slightly oily and often egg-heavy. I was looking for the same sherbet taste but with a real fizz finish. The sorbet provides the same effect that egg white does but is lighter and smoother. This simple modification of one ingredient in an already fantastic recipe results in a perfectly balanced and refreshing fizz.

1. Shake all the ingredients except for the soda in a cocktail tin and strain into a highball or rocks glass.

2. Top with soda water and gently stir. Garnish with an orange slice.

INGREDIENTS
— 50ml gin
— 25ml fresh lemon juice
— 10ml sugar syrup
— 1 scoop of homemade lemon sorbet (page 209)
— Soda water, to top
— Orange slice, to garnish

Sgroppino

1. Combine all the ingredients in a blender and blitz.

2. Pour into a hurricane glass.

INGREDIENTS
— 20ml vodka
— 2 scoops of lemon
  ice cream
— 75ml champagne
  or Prosecco

Elegante [1999]

One of the most interesting elements of taste is how it can trigger memories. For me, summers spent in Sicily are synonymous with drinking Sgroppino. When creating the original menu at Isola in 1999, the Elegante arose from my desire for an elegant blended drink, as those were getting a panning at the time. Inspired by the summery Sgroppino, I decided to make a more refined and refreshing version.

I began by making sorbet and playing with the proportions of vodka. By exchanging the creaminess of ice cream for sorbet and blending the Prosecco, the bubbles break but keep their fizz and this combination makes for a delicious sherbet tang. Over the last decade it has been both a summer favourite and a drink that can be tailored according to the seasons. I have also adapted the recipe with homemade mandarin and raspberry sorbets, both of which add a new dimension to the cocktail.

1. Place all the ingredients in a blender, apart from the lemon, and blend for approximately 30 seconds – a smooth sound indicates that the ice chips are ground.

2. Pour the mix into a coupette and finish by using a stringer to express the oils from the lemon's zest over the drink.

INGREDIENTS
— 50ml vodka
— 25ml fresh lemon juice
— 15ml sugar syrup
— 60ml Prosecco
— 1 scoop of homemade
  lemon sorbet (page 209)
— 1 scoop of crushed ice
  (roughly 150g)
— 1 lemon, for zest garnish

Elegante

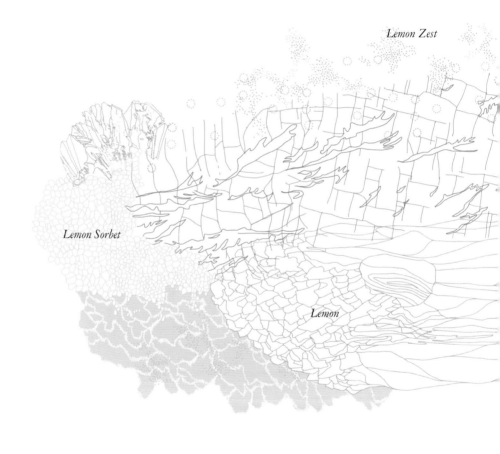

Lemon Zest

Lemon Sorbet

Lemon

FIGURE 1: Elegante – Flavour and Aroma Journey

Prosecco

Sweet Manhattan

1. Combine all the ingredients in a cocktail tin over cubed ice.

2. Stir and then strain into a small, chilled coupette. Garnish with a Marasca cherry.

INGREDIENTS
— 40ml bourbon
— 20ml sweet vermouth
— 2.5ml maraschino
— 3 dashes of
   Angostura bitters
— Marasca cherry,
   to garnish

Vintage Manhattan [2004]

It was after receiving a gift of 1920s Dubonnet that I first became interested in the play between what is 'classic' and what is 'vintage'. I was amazed how good it tasted – the residual air in the bottle had both matured and mellowed the flavours. I was struck by the thought that the evolution of drinks is almost Darwinian: the best ones outlast their competition and many have survived from before the turn of the 20th century. Following the theory of evolution, I then wondered if it was possible to make the best ones even better without just changing the obvious components of product and proportion.

The powerful flavours of the Manhattan made this an ideal candidate for my first experimentation. After reading a number of papers, I was particularly inspired by a piece by Harold McGee, in which he talked about the effect of oxidisation on wine. I wondered if I could use oxidisation in a positive way, controlling the process and thus re-fortifying not only sweet vermouth but also the bourbon.

I started the process using a test batch of different bourbons and vermouths with varying proportions of alcohol, sealing staves inside the bottles and storing them in cupboards. I mixed the Manhattan in a large bowl and poured it into old 700ml bourbon bottles, which were sterilised and dried, making sure that I left an air gap of 2.5cm from the top of

INGREDIENTS
— 450ml rye whisky
— 225ml sweet vermouth
— 200 microns
   Angostura bitters

INGREDIENTS FOR A
SINGLE SERVING
— 50ml Vintage
   Manhattan mix
— 2.5ml maraschino
— Marasca cherry,
   to garnish

the cap and taping the bottle with electrical tape to control oxidisation. I had to ensure a consistent temperature all year round and so left them in a cellar where the sunlight would not be able to penetrate. I tested each bottle after six months but the flavour didn't quite strike the nerve I was after. I left the bottles for a further five months and the flavours they released when tasted were complex, punchy and yet soft – an incredible combination.

In a freshly made Manhattan there is a distinct line where the vermouth begins and the bourbon ends – I find that I can even time this line when drinking. Very much like a young wine, it has fresh, pleasant characteristics. With the aged Manhattan this line dissipates, the flavours collapse in on themselves and the drink becomes unpredictable with a lengthy flavour that reverberates until the last sip.

Continuing with trial and error of different bourbons, vermouths and aging times, I made 48 bottles of Manhattan 2:1 (the ratio of 13-year-old rye whisky to sweet vermouth), with 0.29 of Angostura bitters. I found that the higher the ABV (alcohol by volume) of the rye whisky, the better the process worked, to the point where even after just six months of aging, the Manhattan had a delicious taste. I have opened bottles from this batch each year since 2004. The longer each bottle spends aging, the more its flavours peak and spike as the chemicals of the alcohol react with one another. From one year onwards, all the flavours of the Manhattan are accentuated and fill the mouth; the vermouth feels richer, the bourbon heavier. It makes for an elegant and decadent cocktail with a powerful aroma, which lingers on the glass for hours afterwards. The six-year vintage has an incredibly long finish, enormous body and a gentle hue like a vintage tawny port. Its flavours truly weigh on the tongue – it's a Manhattan with the volume turned all the way up!

1. Mix all the ingredients together and pour into a 700ml bottle, leaving 2.5cm at the top.

2. Tightly seal with a cap and waterproof tape. Leave for a minimum of 6 months in a cool, dark place.

For a single serving:

1. Combine all the ingredients in a cocktail tin and stir over cubed ice.

2. Strain and pour into a small, chilled coupette. Garnish with a Marasca cherry.

Vintage Manhattan

Sazerac

1. Combine all the ingredients except the absinthe over cubed ice in a cocktail tin.

2. Shake and fine-strain into an absinthe-rinsed rocks glass.

INGREDIENTS
— 50ml Rittenhouse Rye
— 10ml sugar syrup
— 3 dashes of
    Peychaud's Bitters
— 15ml absinthe, to
    rinse glass

The Wink ^{2003}

One of the most alluring aspects of the drinking experience is that a bar is an accepted environment in which to indulge in cheeky repartee. The interaction between customer and bartender is extremely important and it inspired this coyly named drink.

Whilst working at the extremely busy Lonsdale House, visiting friends often complained to me that they couldn't get a drink fast enough. A remedy to this malady was found in the form of a surreptitious wink, whereby friends would walk in and wink at me to indicate the number of drinks they desired. Avid gin-drinkers at the time (and still, I'm sure), the wink denoted a form of gin Sazerac. The Peychaud's Bitters and gin complement the orange note that pops up in the middle of the drink and the absinthe rinse on the glass induces a delicious aroma and subtle taste.

When this cocktail later found its way onto menus, it became the waiter or waitress who delivered the wink to the customer as they set the drink down.

1. Combine the gin, triple sec, syrup and bitters over cubed ice in a cocktail tin.

2. Shake and fine-strain into a small, absinthe-rinsed rocks glass. To finish, spritz the orange zest over the drink and discard.

INGREDIENTS
— 40ml gin
— 10ml triple sec
— 15ml sugar syrup
— 2 dashes of
    Peychaud's Bitters
— 15ml absinthe, to
    rinse glass
— Orange twist (page 221),
    to finish

The Wink

Oh Gosh

Daiquiri

1. Combine the ingredients over cubed ice in a cocktail tin.

2. Shake hard and double-strain into a large, chilled coupette. Garnish with a lime wedge on the rim.

INGREDIENTS

— 50ml 3-year-old rum
— 20ml fresh lime juice
— 10ml sugar syrup
— Lime wedge, to garnish

Oh Gosh [2000]

There are moments in bartending that are 'sink or swim' for the bartender, none more so than when a regular customer asks, 'Can you make me something slightly different today?' At Dick's Bar at The Atlantic I had a quintessentially English regular, a brain surgeon by profession, who drank nothing but daiquiris – mostly in large quantities. Having been put on the spot by his unusual request, rather than relying on a repertoire of back-up rum drinks, I decided to take out one shot of rum from the usual daiquiri and replace it with triple sec, garnishing with a lemon twist.

This simple movement resulted in a daiquiri with three levels of citrus: deep orange, tangy lime and a light, zesty, lemon finish. Just after his first sip, the brain surgeon wobbled on his stool and remarked, 'Oh Gosh!' Thus it was christened.

1. Combine the ingredients over cubed ice in a cocktail tin.

2. Shake hard and double-strain into a large, chilled coupette. Finish with a lemon twist.

INGREDIENTS

— 25ml 3-year-old rum
— 25ml triple sec
— 15ml fresh lime juice
— 10ml sugar syrup
— Lemon twist (page 221), to finish

Dry Ice Daiquiri ²⁰¹⁰

Makes 2

Whilst in Cuba, I became engaged in a discussion, lamenting in tone, on how blended daiquiris melt so quickly in the sweltering Cuban climate. I love the texture of a properly blended drink and a truly delicious cocktail will retain both its texture and temperature right until you (sadly) reach the bottom of the glass.

A while before this discussion took place, I had been experimenting with a dry-ice ice cream in classic cocktail flavours. Dry ice freezes the ice cream faster and with smaller crystals, which makes for a smoother ice cream. I couldn't see why the same technique shouldn't work for a daiquiri.

The temperature of the drink is set at -6°C and it stays this cold for the duration of its consumption. A pleasing side effect of this is that the lime takes on a sherbet-like fizz. Whilst being blended, the gas from the dry ice evaporates, which is incredibly theatrical to watch. Once all the gas has dissipated you know that the drink is ready. A few bubbles are left in order to retain a subtle fizzing quality. The ultimate blended daiquiri!

1. Combine all the liquid ingredients in a blender.

2. With the motor running, very slowly and carefully add the dry ice through the hole in the lid (N.B. always wear protective gloves when handling dry ice). Pour into a coupette to serve.

INGREDIENTS
— 100ml Havana Blanco
— 50ml fresh lime juice
— 60ml gomme syrup
— 240ml mineral water
— 100g dry ice

Flintlock ²⁰¹¹

The Flintlock is a complex combination of antique-feeling ingredients. Gunpowder tea was very popular at the turn of the 20th century and, for a green tea, has an incredibly bold flavour. It works in this drink by harmonising with the green tea, whilst the dandelion and burdock bitters adds a touch of anise, mirroring the liquorice present in the gin. Fernet Branca rounds off these flavours with its subtle, herbaceous flavour lingering upon the glass.

The name references the type of gun used at the turn of the century that used flint to ignite gunpowder; the resulting smell of the smoke once the gunpowder is lit also contributes to the drink in both an olfactory and sensory fashion. When serving the drink at the bar, we accompany this with magician's wool (see page 220), set alight at the table as a theatrical extra. When lit, it flames very quickly and then disappears.

1. Add cubed ice to a small rocks glass, along with the Fernet Branca. In a cocktail tin, combine the gin, Gunpowder tincture and bitters, and stir.

2. Discard the Fernet Branca and ice, and strain the drink into the rocks glass. Serve with the magician's wool, set alight alongside the drink.

INGREDIENTS
— 15ml Fernet Branca, to rinse glass
— 50ml London Dry gin
— 15ml Gunpowder tincture (page 188)
— 3 dashes of dandelion and burdock bitters
— Magician's wool (page 220), to serve

Egg Nog

1. Beat the egg yolks with the sugar to form a batter. Add the cream and milk and whisk thoroughly. Continue whisking while adding the bourbon and spiced rum slowly.

2. In a separate bowl, whisk the egg whites until they form stiff peaks, then fold the whites into the batter mix.

3. Serve in a large bowl and ladle into small cups. Sprinkle with grated nutmeg.

INGREDIENTS
— 6 eggs, separated
— 300g sugar
— 600ml single cream
— 1.1 litres whole milk
— 180ml bourbon
— 180ml spiced rum
— 1 tbsp freshly grated nutmeg, to finish

Somerset Egg Nog ²⁰¹⁰

As with food, drink recipes (particularly punch) are passed down via families and friends, with each generation adding its own twists. I first sampled, and then inherited, this recipe from Dale Degroff, who in turn was taught it by his uncle Angelo. Dale's recipe uses bourbon and spiced rum and I exchanged these for cider brandy and cider.

Cider brandy gives this drink a wonderful kick whilst simultaneously adding spice and dryness. The carbonation of the cider makes the mix fluffy. On paper the ingredients suggest a heavy, stocky drink, but the order and method ensure that the end product is light and yielding.

1. Beat the egg yolks with the sugar to form a batter. Add the cream and milk and whisk thoroughly. Continue whisking while slowly adding the cider and cider brandy.

2. In a separate bowl, whisk the egg whites until they form stiff peaks. Fold the whites into the batter mix.

3. Serve in a large bowl and ladle into small cups or glasses.

4. To garnish, grate fresh apple over the drink and top each cup with a sprinkling of grated nutmeg.

INGREDIENTS
— 6 eggs, separated
— 300g sugar
— 300ml single cream
— 600ml whole milk
— 150ml Breton cider
— 150ml 5-year Somerset cider brandy
— Freshly grated apple and nutmeg, to garnish

Somerset Egg Nog

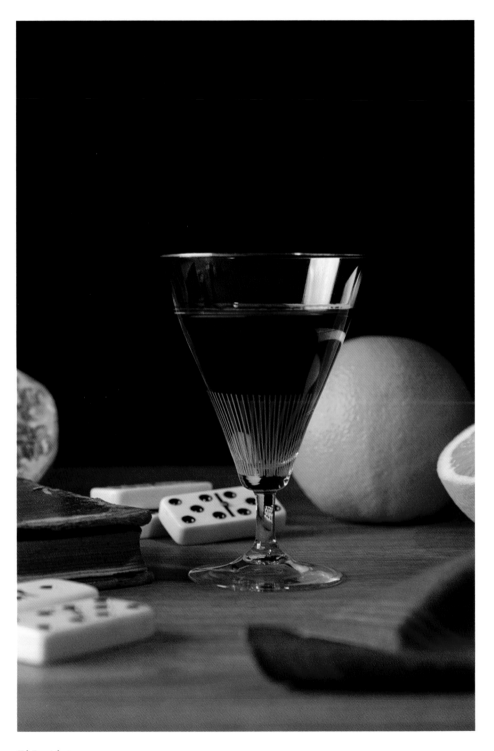

El Presidente

El Presidente

1. Combine all the ingredients in a cocktail tin and stir over cubed ice.

2. Strain into a small, chilled coupette. Finish with an orange twist.

INGREDIENTS
— 40ml Havana
   Barrel Proof
— 20ml sweet vermouth
— 10ml triple sec
— 5ml homemade grenadine
   (page 182)
— Orange twist (page 221),
   to garnish

Consulate 2009

The Cuban classic, El Presidente, is one of my all-time favourite drinks. The cocktail was named in honour of Cuban president Gerardo Machad, who ruled through most of the Prohibition years. Suitably distinguished in nature, this version is a lighter, more summery version of the El Presidente. The peach and sherry notes match the golden rum, and the sherry gently coaxes out the sour facet present in sweet vermouth.

1. Combine all the ingredients in a cocktail tin and stir over cubed ice.

2. Strain into a small, chilled coupette. Finish with an orange twist.

INGREDIENTS
— 40ml golden rum
— 20ml sweet vermouth
— 10ml fino sherry
— 5ml crème de pêche
— Orange twist (page 221),
   to garnish

Ramos Gin Fizz

1. Combine all the ingredients in a cocktail shaker with a splash of Vichy Catalan.

2. Shake vigorously over cubed ice until there is no ice whatsoever left in the shaker.

3. Strain into a highball glass and top with Vichy Catalan.

INGREDIENTS
— 45ml gin
— 25ml single cream
— 25ml egg white
— 25ml sugar syrup
— 15ml fresh lemon juice
— 15ml fresh lime juice
— 5ml maraschino
— 2 dashes of orange blossom water
— Vichy Catalan sparkling water, to top

Almond Ramos 2007

Yield: 2

Ferran Adrià's foray into foams demonstrates how to crown a drink with a frothy foam that endures until the very last sip. I wanted to use this technology to replicate the texture of a classic Ramos but with a lighter feel.

To do this, I replaced the dairy element of the original recipe with *latte di mandorla* – the Italian almond milk I used to drink as a child. This is great for those who prefer their drinks without dairy. The pairing of almond and maraschino cherry is a classic combination in the pastry world and it works equally well here in liquid form.

The foam, produced by a siphon, traps flavour, both aerating and accentuating it for an incredibly light drink without any compromising punch. Fans of the Almond Ramos say it tastes like a cloud – they may have had one too many…

1. Add all the ingredients to an ISI siphon charged with an N2O gas charger.

2. Chill in the fridge for 30 minutes or until cooled.

3. Release the foam by pressing the lever and pour into a Ramos glass.

INGREDIENTS
— 60g Beefeater gin
— 25g egg white
— 15g lemon juice
— 15g lime juice
— 10g sugar syrup
— 5g maraschino
— 0.5g orange blossom water
— 212g almond milk (page 171)
— 1 N2O gas charger

Almond Ramos

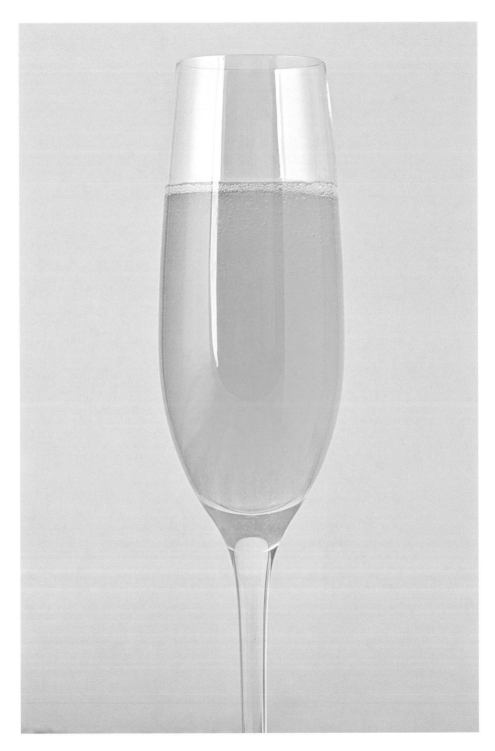

Rhubarb Royale

Kir Royale

1. Build in a champagne flute and gently stir to mix.

INGREDIENTS
— 15ml cassis
— 115ml champagne

Rhubarb Royale

Ordering a Royale before dinner in France will present you with an abundance of tantalising options. Rather than limiting themselves to using only cassis, the French offer such liqueurs as crème de mûre, poire or framboise as a delicious addition to a glass of champagne.

I took this as inspiration for a more British take on the Kir Royale. I combined a homemade British rhubarb cordial with rhubarb liqueur, finishing off with Nyetimber – a fantastic English sparkling wine. Rhubarb and sparkling wine are a great marriage: the beautiful rose colour gives way to the dryness of the wine, allowing the slight tartness of the rhubarb to really shine through. The result is a minimal and delicious aperitif – a perfect start to the evening.

1. Build in a 150ml champagne flute and gently stir to mix.

INGREDIENTS
— 15ml rhubarb cordial
   (page 168)
— 15ml rhubarb liqueur
   (page 182)
— 115ml English sparkling
   wine (Nyetimber)

New York Sour

1. Combine the bourbon, lemon juice, egg white and sugar syrup in a cocktail tin.

2. Dry-shake, then shake over cubed ice. Strain and pour into a large, chilled coupette.

3. Pour in the claret last (this avoids aerating and diluting the flavour of the wine through shaking).

INGREDIENTS
— 50ml bourbon
— 25ml fresh lemon juice
— 25ml egg white
— 15ml sugar syrup
— 10ml claret

Spitfire 2010

I have always enjoyed a New York or Boston Sour – bourbon sours with a claret or port float – but neither was a drink that I particularly felt like having in the summer. I was after a lighter version for balmy evenings and began by matching a cognac sour with a peach liqueur that would draw out the fruity element present in cognac. In turn, I wanted to dry out and lengthen the flavour of peach whilst ensuring it wasn't too sweet. I added white wine, purposely choosing an Ugni Blanc, which is made from the same grape as cognac and mirrors its slight peachy notes.

The 69 Colebrooke Row house cognac was formulated with the Spitfire in mind. Gilles and son Luc of the Merlet family are long-term associates of mine. I went to them to create a cognac that was drinkable in itself but with a bounty of fruity notes that would sit underneath the peach flavour. In response, they sent me eight samples with tasting notes. I tasted each of these on their own, made a range of classic cocktails and finally used them in a Spitfire.

The Spitfire changed the way I think about the structure of cocktails. At first glance this drink seems to combine ingredients that don't appear to work together. However, the framework of a cocktail recipe has a formula just like a sheet of music. You can take this formula and play it in one key but it will also work if you play it in a higher or lower key. It was with this in mind that I was able to achieve an incredible harmony of flavours where the peach acts as a bridge between all the ingredients.

INGREDIENTS
— 40ml cognac
— 25ml fresh lemon juice
— 25ml egg white
— 15ml sugar syrup
— 10ml crème de pêche
— 25ml dry white wine

1. Combine the cognac, lemon juice, egg white, sugar syrup and crème de pêche in a cocktail tin.

2. Dry-shake and then shake over cubed ice. Strain into a large, chilled coupette and pour in the dry white wine last (this avoids aerating and diluting the flavour of the wine through shaking).

Spitfire

2.
CULINARY SKILLS

Introduction _____

Culinary Skills

For a long time there has been a blatant divide between the two crafts of food and drink. The last few years have witnessed the record development of a more open exchange between chefs and bartenders in a way that was previously only experienced by sommeliers. The psychology and physiology of the two professions are of course different, but they have an undeniable overlap. Both consider sensitivity of the mouth and the way that flavour works, and both forever seek new ingredients, methods and processes to release, revive, and reinforce flavour.

Over the years I have developed a long-standing relationship with the chef Bruno Loubet, which began in 1998 whilst working at the restaurant and bar Isola. This meeting of minds marked the beginning of my first bout of real creative freedom. It was during this time that I developed an interest in watching pastry chefs and the way they manipulated ingredients, particularly in the making of purées and utilising the flavour profiles of fruit and vegetables. I ceased simply looking through the lens of a bartender, broadening the spectrum of ingredients that I worked with.

At this time, seasonality was a new way of thinking and a novel enterprise. I began to visit farmers' markets and build relationships with individual farmers; this ensured that the fruit I was using had never been frozen and had no travelling time. The farmers would call me with news of seasonal stock and then I'd buy directly from them. This was a unique idea for cocktail-making. Since then, a new era has dawned in which chefs are now paying attention to drink more than ever before, and now cocktails have even arrived in three-Michelin-star restaurants. Chefs have led the way in the past, but our project as bartenders is different; for a long time it has been my aim to branch out from where they began.

Although I continue to employ chefs' techniques and utilise the skills of the culinary world, I reached a certain point where I realised that the focus should be on creating our own bartending language. The time that a drink actually spends in your mouth is much shorter than the longevity of a chewed ingredient and there is less repeated retronasal; therefore the opportunity a bartender has to execute flavour is very narrow. The fact that texture is also minimal means that we are relying almost entirely on a perception of flavour – it's like we are taking the sense of touch out of flavour, or separating the sense of touch.

The following drink recipes trace the progress made from the very beginning of my relationship with chefs and fruit suppliers, going on to explore a new awareness in working with seasonality and translating this to function practically within the bar world.

Chefs have led the way in the past, but our project as bartenders is different; for a long time it has been my aim to branch out from where they began.

Sweet Grilled Lemon Margarita ¹⁹⁹⁸

This simple twist on a classic margarita is the brainchild of my first foray into observing the cooking techniques of chefs. Grilling the lemon relieves the fruit of its acid bite by caramelising the fructose and killing its vitamin C.

The flavour of the lemon after juicing takes on a delicious, deep, sultry, caramel note that makes it a perfect match for the caramel and toffee notes found in a reposado tequila. I like to use a dry triple sec, such as Merlet, to balance the sweetness of the grilled lemon with a dry finish. This version of the margarita has an incredible, smooth and soft finish, making it hard to have only one!

1. Combine all the ingredients except the sugar in a cocktail tin and shake over cubed ice.

2. Fine-strain and pour into a chilled coupette with a half sugar rim.

INGREDIENTS

— 50ml reposado tequila
— 25ml grilled lemon juice (page 164)
— 20ml triple sec
— Sugar, for the rim

Sweet Grilled Lemon Margarita

Apple Mojito

Apple Mojito [1999]

For a bartender, serving cocktails every day, rather than consuming them, can leave you hankering for more than just water for refreshment. I began playing around with fruit juices, hoping for something more flavourful and invigorating. I found that a great way of achieving this is simply to exchange the rum in a mojito with freshly pressed apple juice.

There are heaps of detox properties in every element of this drink. As a whole, the three major components are fantastic for facilitating and improving digestion. In addition, lime juice works hard to rejuvenate the skin, apples aid in preventing anaemia and weakness, and mint helps with both headaches and nausea and activates the saliva glands to promote taste.

For those not drinking alcohol, habitually or exceptionally, there's no reason not to be drinking something really good. This is simple to make, especially in batches. Of course, when good intentions fail, simply substitute the apple juice for a delicious dark rum!

1. Muddle the mint sprigs with the sugar syrup in a cocktail tin.

2. Mix in the lemon and lime juices, then add crushed ice and the apple juice.

3. Shake twice and then pour the mixture into a highball glass.

4. Garnish with a lemon and lime slice and a bruised mint sprig.

INGREDIENTS
— 6 mint sprigs
— 15ml sugar syrup
— 10ml fresh lemon juice
— 15ml fresh lime juice
— 75ml freshly pressed green apple juice
— Lemon and lime slice and mint sprig, to garnish

Gooseberry and Elderflower Collins ¹⁹⁹⁹

Few drinks are as refreshing as the Tom Collins on a summer's afternoon, and this version began life as a platform for the delicious – but unfortunately short-lived – gooseberry season, which lasts for just two to three weeks in August.

The gooseberry resonates with a sharp and sour tang and this is balanced by the acidity of the lemon and the deep, mellow flavour of the elderflower. Originally made with gooseberry syrup, over time technology (and multiple trials and errors) led to the discovery that homemade cordials worked much better in many cocktails – this one included. The cordial has the same proportions as the syrup, combining sugar, water and elderflower, but has a much fresher and cleaner finish.

The first batch of gooseberry gin I made was 35 litres and I thought this would last a long time. However, it sold extremely quickly and I had to wait an entire year to make the next batch!

1. In a highball glass, build the gooseberry gin, lemon juice and elderflower cordial over cubed ice.

2. Gently stir with a bar spoon.

3. Finish with soda, and garnish with a lemon wedge and a gooseberry.

INGREDIENTS
— 50ml gooseberry gin (page 210)
— 25ml fresh lemon juice
— 20ml homemade elderflower cordial (page 169)
— Soda water, to top
— Lemon wedge and single gooseberry, to garnish

Gooseberry and Elderflower Collins

Fig and Liquorice Caipirinha

Fig and Liquorice Caipirinha

Ploughing through the pastry books in the kitchen at Isola, I was occupied by a constant search for fresh flavour combinations. Rather than simply turning to classic cocktails and cocktail books, for the first time I began to research classical desserts for inspiration.

I uncovered an old pastry recipe that used fig and liquorice and I began to translate this combination back to the bartending world. Although the lifespan of the fig is very short, it's well worth using fresh figs in this recipe; fig syrups or liqueurs never fully replicate the flavour of real fig. The flavour links between the cachaça, fig and liquorice are made in heaven.

1. Muddle all the ingredients in a cocktail tin and add crushed ice.

2. Shake briskly and pour into a rocks glass. Garnish with a fig slice.

INGREDIENTS
— 50ml cachaça
— 1 lime, cut into 8 wedges
— 1 ripe fig, skinned and cut into 8 pieces
— 15ml liquorice syrup
— Fig slice, to garnish

Fruit Gin and Tonics ²⁰⁰⁵

Bitter Lemon, Grapefruit, Raspberry, Blood Orange

Working with fruit in cocktails pivots upon two factors: the quality of the fruit and the process by which you combine it with the alcohol. I was dissatisfied with the off-note often produced by macerating fruit; I wanted a truly fresh flavour – a super-clean imprint of the fruit onto the alcohol. I observed the way in which pastry chefs cook fruit sous vide and could see no reason why this principle couldn't also be applied to cooking fruit with alcohol.

The sous vide method (page 148) is essentially cooking at a low, controlled and constant temperature using a water bath. Cooking in this way transports the flavour from the fruit to the gin incredibly effectively. The gin is placed into vacuum bags with the fruit and sealed. I never add any sugar as this unbalances the tonic. The alcohol is infused at a low temperature, which ensures that the structure doesn't fall apart. Controlling the temperature is important. If the temperature exceeds 52°C, the heat pulls apart the structure of the alcohol. The closed system allows cooking to take place without oxygen; this way the volatiles don't evaporate and none of the flavour or moisture is lost.

Audrey Saunders, dear friend and queen of the New York cocktail scene, inspired me with her recipe for bitter lemon gin. I began my own version by infusing gin with lemon peel. It works wonderfully in a stark drink such as the gin and tonic because the flavour can take centre stage. It's important to use a gin that will stand up for itself otherwise the fruit will overpower its complexities. It was a lengthy process to find the right balance between fruit and gin quantities; each fruit has its own point at which the best flavour match with the gin is obtained – and each fruit balances in a different way with the tonic. Fruit fibres have to be fine-strained else the gin will keep changing its flavour. This can be done in a Büchner funnel.

1. Build the gin and tonic water over cubed ice and garnish with the corresponding fruit.

INGREDIENTS
— 50ml fruit gin (see pages 199–202 and 210)
— 150ml tonic water
— Fruit, to garnish

(Clockwise from top left) Bitter Lemon, Grapefruit, Blood Orange and Raspberry Gins

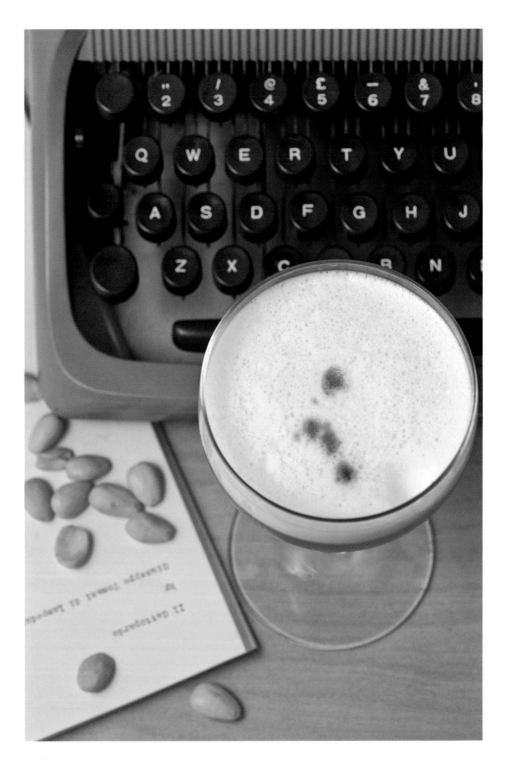

Sicilian Sour

Sicilian Sour ²⁰⁰⁶

In 1998, my grandmother's recipe book was unearthed. Its discovery revealed an incredible series of recipes for homemade liqueurs such as limoncello, crème de cacao and amaretto. The amaretto recipe leapt out at me, comprised as it was of entirely natural ingredients. I loved the idea of using my grandmother's recipe in a cocktail that would be an honour both to her and to my family's Sicilian history.

My abiding memories of being a child in Sicily, other than the freedom of running around in the sunshine, are of flavours and scents. To recapture summers past, I called upon almonds, apricots and lemons – a tasty triangle of Italian ingredients native to Sicily. Apricot pits and almond kernels are very similar and amaretto can be made from both. Amaretto has a bitter, as well as a sweet, note that is often overlooked, and this is complemented by the Angostura bitters. Using ingredients that inspire a different and drier tonality to amaretto, the Sicilian Sour is a delicious twist on a well-known drink.

1. Add all ingredients except the bitters and lemon slice to a cocktail tin.

2. Dry-shake, then shake over cubed ice. Strain into a large, chilled coupette.

3. Garnish with a dash of bitters and a lemon slice on the edge of the glass, if liked.

INGREDIENTS
— 35ml homemade amaretto (page 181)
— 15ml apricot liqueur
— 25ml fresh lemon juice
— 25ml egg white
— 5ml sugar syrup
— Dash of Angostura bitters
— Lemon slice, to garnish (optional)

Marshmallow Milkshake ²⁰⁰⁶

I love milkshakes that are soft, foamy and light. I spent some time looking at a history of American flavours and tried to utilise them in the milkshake format. The homemade mallow syrup really brings out the true earthy, woody and creamy flavour of mallow – so much more delicious than the synthetic options. Using a siphon makes the mixture lighter and softer than using a blender. The result is a super-subtle set of flavours with a comforting moreishness to them.

1. Put all the ingredients into an ISI siphon charged with an N2O gas charger.

2. Release the milkshake by pressing down on the lever, pour into a vintage milk bottle and serve with a straw.

INGREDIENTS

— 70ml mallow syrup (page 180)
— 200ml single cream
— 200ml whole milk
— 1 N2O gas charger

Marshmallow Milkshake

Sous Vide Fruit Bellini [2004]

Giuseppe Cipriani, the founder of the infamous Harry's Bar in Venice, created the Bellini around the time of the Second World War. His recipe was simply white peach purée topped with Prosecco. Cipriani named his drink in honour of the Venetian painter Giovanni Bellini because its peachy, fleshy hue matched the skin tones used in his work. He always stirred the Prosecco and the purée together, as I do here, which means you achieve an integrated drink with a rich foam.

Since its inception, the Bellini has enjoyed enduring popularity for the simple way it packs in flavour, and for being refreshing and glamorous in equal measure. Although wine can be a complex ingredient to work with, its low ABV broadens the space for flavour to really shine through and the versatility of Prosecco also makes it ideal for fruits other than peach. It is important, however, to allow the integrity of the Prosecco to remain by pairing it with a fruit that can sit within the framework of the Prosecco without masking its flavours, such as the suggestions that follow.

Working in accordance with the seasons means that I am constantly discovering new combinations of flavours and updating my recipe book. Good-quality fresh fruit is vital but you can freeze your purées if you want.

1. First pour the purée into a cocktail tin, then add the Prosecco.

2. Stir very gently so as not to burst the bubbles in the Prosecco. Strain into a champagne flute or tumbler.

INGREDIENTS
— 50ml peach purée
— 100ml Prosecco

1. First pour the purée into a cocktail tin, then add the Prosecco.

2. Stir very gently so as not to burst the bubbles in the Prosecco. Strain into a champagne flute or tumbler.

INGREDIENTS
— (see opposite and pages 204–5)
— 100ml Prosecco

Wild Strawberry and Neroli

This recipe began life as a foodie joke but soon became one of my favourite Bellini combinations. It was Hervé This who first showed me that the chemical difference between strawberries and wild strawberries can be imitated by adding lemon juice, orange blossom water and sugar.

To the 'wild' strawberry purée I added a hint of neroli, an essential oil derived from orange blossom. The strawberry, neroli and Prosecco all share a chemical overlap that creates an incredible flow of flavours. See the purée recipe on page 204.

Cherry Blossom and Almond

The acidity level of cherries can be hard to regulate, making a good purée difficult. To remedy this, once the purée is made I check the acidity with a Brix meter (see page 160) and a pH level meter. The resulting Bellini is fruity, tart and juicy with a subtle hint of marzipan. See the purée recipe on page 205.

Pear and Green Tea

I love the flavour of Williams pears, which have a fantastic juiciness and are a brilliant match for the flavours of Prosecco. It is important to use a very high-quality Japanese matcha powder. This slight Japanese twist on the Bellini was first made at the restaurant Roka, and has a delicious juicy/dry dichotomy alongside a slightly tannic finish. See the purée recipe on page 205.

Pumpkin

Using this vegetable in a cocktail sounds a little off-key, but the pumpkin purée is an incredible match for Prosecco, with a vivid orange hue. See the purée recipe on page 204.

Pictured overleaf

Sous Vide Fruit Bellinis

Nettle Gimlet ²⁰¹⁰

Britain has a long history of earthy, simple, tasty cuisine. The national flavour psyche of beetroot, nettle, cabbage, dandelion and sorrel has recently experienced a justly deserved revival in popularity. I tentatively ordered nettle, leek and goat's curd soup at a restaurant in Soho recently, unsure of what to expect but anticipating the worst! The only experience I'd really had with nettles was falling into a giant bed of them when I was young. Putting this to one side, I dived in and it was fantastic – not at all what I had expected!

I took advantage of this renaissance of British flavour and created a twist on the classic Gimlet using traditional dried nettles. I looked at nettle cordial recipes that dated back to the 1800s and realised how simply they could be made. I tried recipes with both fresh and dried nettles, but the dried produced a range of beautiful tannic notes. I use a dehydrator to dry the leaves, but you could just as easily turn the nettles upside down and dry them by a window.

The resulting cordial is surprisingly fruity and reminiscent of elderflowers. The grassy flavour of nettles works well with the orris root, angelica and juniper botanicals in gin. The subtleties of the spirit are left undiminished and are complemented rather than softened by the fruitiness of the cordial.

The Nettle Gimlet is quirky yet grown-up – a conceptual but very drinkable re-imagining of the Gimlet proper.

1. Combine the gin and cordial in a cocktail tin and stir over cubed ice.

2. Strain into a small, chilled coupette and finish with a small lemon twist.

INGREDIENTS
— 40ml gin
— 20ml nettle cordial (page 169)
— Lemon twist (page 221), to finish

Nettle Gimlet

Rhubarb Gimlet ²⁰¹¹

The natural progression of my interest in the Gimlet remained British in nature and continued to work in accordance with the seasons. I love rhubarb for its complex set of flavours which loans itself to a broad spectrum of cocktails, and in particular rhubarb and gin are a perfect match. The Rhubarb Gimlet is a cocktail with a neat circle of flavours; simple, pared down and minimal, with a seasonal twist.

1. Combine the gin and cordial in a cocktail tin and stir over cubed ice.

2. Strain into a small, chilled coupette.

3. Finish with a grapefruit twist.

INGREDIENTS
— 40ml gin
— 20ml homemade rhubarb cordial (page 168)
— Grapefruit twist, to finish

Somerset Sour ²⁰⁰⁹

Creating a cocktail that can be enjoyed during a specific season is a real driving force behind many of my recipes. If the Spitfire is a more summery version of a New York Sour, then the Somerset Sour does the same for autumn. For me, autumn time is epitomised by the flavours and aromas associated with Halloween: the smell of hay, toffee and bobbing apples. I wanted to encapsulate these in a drink and in doing so orchestrate a shared nostalgia of autumn for every drinker.

Cider brandy is distilled at autumn time and although it was an ingredient that I had never worked with before, I chose it as the base of this cocktail because it really captures the taste of apples at this time of year. The layering of ingredients was as important to this Sour as in the Spitfire; adding cognac dries out the cider brandy whilst introducing an element of toffee-like richness; the cider float ensures a crisp and refreshing finish. I discovered that the food-grade essence CIS-3-Hexenal had the perfect 'just-cut grass' note that, when added to fresh apple, makes it taste and smell just like hay.

During the process of putting together this drink, I was always aware that an apple slice would be a complementary garnish. However, when experimenting with how to stop the apple from browning, it occurred to me that the scoops of apples I was testing would look just like bobbing apples if they were floating in the foam on the Sour. I began by using a melon baller to scoop a variety of apples until I discovered one with the best absorbing qualities – the Pink Lady. If the CIS-3-Hexenal is added with pectin and sorbic acid then the apple is prevented from browning. The resulting apples are incredibly juicy but also crisp from the pectin and acid, with a faint aroma of hay. The mini bobbing apples float in the foam of the Sour to create a garnish that both parallels the flavours of the drink but also enhances them with a multidimensional and multi-sensory flavour experience. This really expands upon the idea of what a garnish can be.

INGREDIENTS
— 40ml cider brandy
— 10ml cognac
— 25ml fresh lemon juice
— 25ml hay-infused egg white (see overleaf)
— 15ml sugar syrup
— Dash of cider
— Bobbing apple (page 211), to garnish

Continues overleaf

Somerset Sour

Aroma was a motivating factor behind this drink. Audrey Saunders and I have often lamented the unfortunate wet-dog-nose smell that arises from egg white reacting with alcohol. Together we have engaged in many conversations about how to eliminate it for good. I had a eureka moment when making truffle omelettes at home. I realised that the truffle flavoured the eggs through scent. Quite simply, since eggs are porous they can absorb smells, and with this as the case, I could use any number of smells to flavour them. All that was needed was to create a controlled environment in which to flavour the eggs through aroma.

I conducted tests by soaking different food-grade hydrosols into cotton wool and sealing them in Tupperware with the eggs, keeping the box in the fridge. The aroma in the box then fills all the empty space, including seeping through the egg shell, which is semi-permeable, meaning it will absorb small molecules around it, and literally adding flavour to the egg itself. With this knowledge I added to the egg white the same hay essence as I had injected into the bobbing apple.

1. Combine all the ingredients except the cider and bobbing apple in a cocktail tin.

2. Dry-shake then shake over cubed ice. Strain and serve in a large, chilled coupette, floating the cider on top.

3. Garnish with hay-infused bobbing apple.

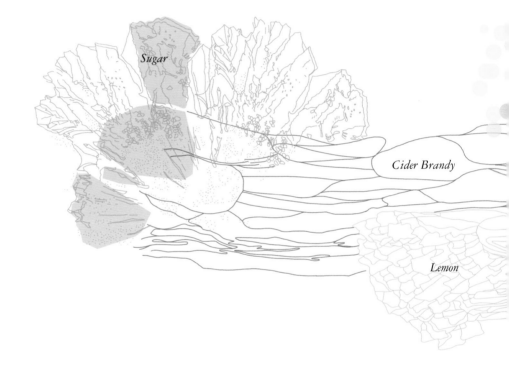

FIGURE 2: Somerset Sour – Flavour and Aroma Journey

Cider

Hay

Egg White

Lime Plus + ²⁰¹⁰

This drink began life as a technical project to examine how lime flavour works. Lime is an integral ingredient in a multitude of cocktail recipes, yet in this country achieving continuity of flavour is often problematic as citrus fruits have to be imported from different parts of the globe. This means that the fruit has variants of sweetness and pH levels and this can affect the consistency of a cocktail over time.

Enabling a uniformity of lime flavour whilst retaining a natural finish to the drink was no simple task, but the final result was one of extraordinary impact. I achieved a deep and multi-layered lime flavour with a lime pressé food-grade essential oil. This is married with homogenised lime juice for maximum flavour.

I added the lime essence directly to the cachaça in minute amounts using a micron pipette, which allowed the lime flavour to really sing through the spirit. An addition of 35 microns of Salivating Mix (page 220) came a little later; it works to stimulate taste buds by increasing salivation, in turn amplifying the flavours of the drink. Waves and layers of lime reveal themselves in new forms as the drink is consumed.

1. Combine all the ingredients in a cocktail tin. Dry-shake, then shake over cubed ice.

2. Strain into a large, chilled whisky glass, twist the lime zest over and discard.

INGREDIENTS
— 50ml Leblon cachaça
— 30ml fresh lime juice
— 25ml egg white
— 15ml sugar syrup
— Lime essence (page 191)
— Lime twist (page 221), to finish

Lime Plus +

3.
SAVOURY

Savoury

Modern drinking culture has substantiated the consumer's tendency to drink things that are sweet, especially during the latter part of the twentieth century. Drinking has long been associated with partying and therefore with sugar – nature's rocket fuel. The last decade has given birth to a growing interest in and understanding about flavour – both at consumer and trade level. I've witnessed a massive increase in the consumption of more savoury drinks like the Negroni and Martini, and that is entirely down to customers understanding more about the way that they drink and challenging their own preconceptions. You don't need to have disco drinks to have fun!

This has perhaps helped the cocktail world to experience a recent savoury revolution, reaching for botanicals and flavours that have been criminally overlooked for a long time. Appealing to the savoury palate calls for a total overhaul of the ingredients most often employed, and especially for a reassessment of sugar content. For a bartender, the parameters of working with a savoury drink are therefore both interesting and challenging.

My interest in savoury cocktails was first awakened by working in a number of bars that were linked to high-profile restaurants, and although this was never intentional, it's a circumstance I have always embraced. It has allowed me to see how cocktails work in a different context and with a different clientele. In restaurants, accuracy reaches new heights of importance; it is not just necessary for the drink to have balance within itself, but also with the food that is being consumed.

Food works on a different level and flavour boundaries change accordingly. I have always had a problem with specific cocktail and food pairing, as more often than not it ends up being a case of trying to force cocktails on food, and vice versa. Whenever I have designed drinks for restaurant menus I make sure that I take the food menu into account, but I have rarely designed cocktails with specific dishes in mind. Whilst the spirituous end of cocktails can be far too strong to continue drinking through a meal, the sourness or sweetness of drinks can rip through the more delicate nuances of food. Therefore, I have always made sure that the cocktails I create are in smaller portions – no one can drink several normal-sized cocktails throughout the course of a meal, even if they really practise! Rather, I like to provide snippets of drinks that can enhance a menu, always taking into consideration how the chefs have thought out the food menu.

Doing this is usually a very long process, constantly tasting and re-tasting but this practice has led to the creation of some of my favourite drinks. The following cocktails are drinks that either have been designed to be consumed with food or were inspired by using savoury ingredients in a new way.

Appealing to the savoury palate calls for a total overhaul of the ingredients most often employed.

White Truffle Martini [1999]

The White Truffle Martini was the first drink I ever created with the sole purpose of working within a savoury stricture. With the Bloody Mary the reigning go-to of savoury drinks, I wanted to open up the parameters of flavour combinations without creating a drink that would only have a niche appeal.

The Martini is a dry drink and accordingly lends itself well to a savoury spin. White truffles have a delicious, decadent flavour, and combining them with dry vermouth plays upon both ingredients' earthy qualities. I made a julienne of the truffles and added just 1g of this to a bottle of vermouth, letting it macerate for one month. The same method can be used with black truffles but requires twice the amount of truffle and leaving it in the bottle for three months. The bottle should be full, sealed both with tape and a cap to avoid oxidisation as much as possible, and then left in the fridge.

The white truffle is a luxurious and sensual product; adding it to an already stylish and graceful drink created an accessible Martini with a new layered profile. Originally conceived whilst working in an Italian restaurant, the White Truffle Martini proved to be extremely popular, especially as an aperitif.

1. Combine your choice of gin or vodka with the vermouth in a cocktail tin and stir over cubed ice.

2. Strain into a small, chilled coupette and garnish with a truffle shaving.

Variation: Black Truffle Martini

Simply replace the white truffle vermouth with black truffle vermouth (page 197).

INGREDIENTS
— 50ml gin or 60ml vodka
— 15ml white truffle vermouth (page 197)
— Truffle shaving, to garnish

Black Truffle Martini

Luna

Luna [2003]

The Luna was invented in collaboration with Ian Wisniewski, the renowned drinks writer and vodka expert. The idea was to create a new profile for the vodka Martini but with already-existing vodkas, resulting in our 'own blend'. We began by conducting numerous in-depth vodka tastings and subsequently matched two for an interesting yet cohesive blend that would also lend itself to the vermouth.

Siwucha is a raw vodka, meaning that it is an incompletely rectified mix of two grain spirits. The mixture is then seasoned in oak barrels and a scent of forest-fruit is added. I particularly like how the earthiness of the Siwucha underpins the drink. It adds incredible complexities: varying musky and residual fusel oil (potato oil) notes.

The Moskovskaya vodka brings fresh mint and anise notes to the equation, which are enhanced by the vermouth and then lengthened by the bitters. There is a profound progression of notes, executed in a very simple way that gives you far more to hold on to than with your average vodka Martini. Collaborations with experts in their field bring an interesting outside perspective, which can really refresh what we do as bartenders.

1. Combine all the ingredients in a cocktail tin and stir over cubed ice.

2. Strain into a chilled coupette, and finish with a lemon twist.

INGREDIENTS
— 40ml Moskovskaya vodka
— 20ml Siwucha vodka
— 10ml dry vermouth
— 1 dash of Angostura bitters
— Lemon twist (page 221), to finish

Noshino ²⁰⁰⁴

The cocktail enthusiast David Embury has written that
the key to a perfectly executed cocktail is that the base,
and what happens around the base, is the direction that
the drink should take. Embury believed that a great drink
should whet rather than dull the appetite; should be dry
with sufficient alcoholic flavour yet smooth and pleasing to
both the palate and the eye. Whilst working at the Shochu
Lounge, I wanted to create an aperitif designed specifically
with Japanese cuisine in mind but keeping in line with
Embury's requirements. Shochu and sake reside in the same
flavour band and together provide the base of this cocktail;
the customer has the option of two garnishes – samphire or
cucumber – which send the drink in opposite directions, in
the same way that an olive or a twist will to a Martini.

Azure sake is made with deep-sea water collected from a
natural spring located at the bottom of the Pacific Ocean,
and it has a subtle, salty quality to it. The samphire garnish
not only aesthetically replicates the seaweed in Japanese
cooking, but also plays to its saltiness. The cucumber
option is much lighter, with a refreshing finish. I wanted to
emulate the cut of sashimi for a complementary aesthetic
and so carefully observed the Head of Sashimi whilst at
work at the Shochu Lounge. He taught me how to use a
sashimi knife correctly: rather than using the wrist in an
up-and-down motion, cutting sashimi requires a sweeping,
pulling-back action. I spent days cutting cucumbers,
looking for the same sharp and angular lines.

This drink has simple ingredients, simple inflections
of flavour and an elegant aesthetic. Minimal and
incredibly drinkable!

1. Combine the shochu and sake in a cocktail tin and stir
over cubed ice.

2. Strain and pour into a sake glass. Garnish with either a
cucumber slice or a strand of samphire.

INGREDIENTS
— 50ml Kigo shochu
— 25ml Azure sake
— Cucumber slice or
    samphire strand,
    to garnish

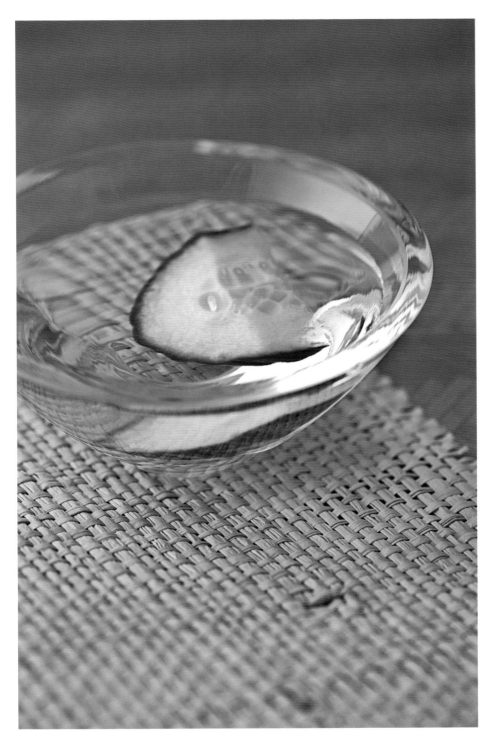

Noshino

The Dry Martini ²⁰⁰⁷

The modern Martini is synonymous with 'dryness', which indicates a small amount of vermouth added to the base spirit. The popularity of this style derives from the way we taste and use our mouth when drinking. The alcohol, herbs and botanicals in both vermouth and gin provide a slight dryish feeling in your mouth. The mouth reacts to this and produces saliva, and in turn the stimulation of the saliva glands prepares your stomach for the prospect of food, producing that hungry feeling.

I wanted to take this process further. It occurred to me that by seeking out ingredients that stimulate dryness, I could then add those ingredients to the drink to enhance the dry sensation. This way, I wouldn't just be playing around with the structure of the Martini. Rather, I was after an ingredient that had no flavour of its own, which could change the cocktail in a simultaneously subtle and dramatic way whilst remaining true to classical proportions.

I spent a lot of time researching exactly how the tongue works and how flavours work once in the mouth. In order to taste, saliva breaks down the components of ingredients. I discovered that tannins and polyphenols, which are normally found in red wine and tea, work to shrink the protein chains in saliva. Grapes have a high content of tannins and polyphenols and by extracting these I could make a tincture that would directly enhance the dryness that is already present in the vermouth. I peeled, dried and made a concentrate of the skins and added a small amount to a bottle of vermouth. I later discovered that the presence of tannins and polyphenols is higher in the grape-seeds and changed the tincture accordingly.

By adding this non-tasting 'dry essence tincture' (page 186), I was able to imbue the Dry Martini with a profundity that gives such depth and length that the drink becomes an entirely different experience. Carefully balanced, the dry essence tincture is not offensively dry, but rather it intensifies flavour by creating a closed circuit of taste in

INGREDIENTS
— 50ml gin
— 15ml 'Dry' dry vermouth (opposite and page 186)
— Green Sicilian olive, to garnish

by creating a closed circuit of taste in the mouth – an incredible flavour loop that keeps going until you reach the juicy green olive waiting for you in the bottom of the glass.

1. Combine the gin and vermouth in a cocktail tin and stir over cubed ice.

2. Strain and pour into a small, chilled coupette. Garnish with a green Sicilian olive.

The Dry Martini

Dirty Martini by the Sea

Dirty Martini by the Sea ²⁰⁰⁸

The Dirty Martini by the Sea was created for a dinner event at Pontus Frithiof, Stockholm, which brought together chefs and sommeliers to pair a small drinks menu with a range of original dishes. This version of a Dirty Martini uses Japanese seaweed cooked sous vide with vodka (page 203) and was created to match a seaweed and oyster dish named the 'Rock Pool'.

I took the same slivers of purple seaweed as were used in the dish and cooked them sous vide with vodka to develop a beautiful purple tint. Using vodka rather than gin really allows the seaweed and vermouth to shine through in this cocktail. A later version had an intense olive bread crisp as a garnish. With the help of a chef I baked some olive bread, froze the loaf and then used a meat-slicer to cut it into thins. Each thin slice was then put back into the oven to heat through. The drink is served in a sake glass and works as a fantastic palate cleanser.

1. Combine the vodka and vermouth in a cocktail tin and stir over cubed ice.

2. Strain and pour into a chilled, small coupette, adding the olive. If liked, serve with crisp olive bread at the side of the glass.

INGREDIENTS
— 50ml seaweed vodka
(page 203)
— 10ml vermouth
— 1 baby Greek olive
— Crisp olive bread,
to serve (optional)

Dirty Martini

The Dirty Martini can be a great drink but a lot of olive brines can be really dreadful. Rather than representing the olive flavour, the brine is often simply oily, salty water. I wanted to create a more refined olive taste that would complement the botanicals in gin rather than just dominating its taste with salt. The result is an incredibly subtle, almost creamy olive flavour that really complements the more savoury characteristics of a good London dry gin.

1. Combine all the ingredients in a cocktail tin and stir over cubed ice.

2. Strain and pour into a chilled, small coupette. Garnish with two green Sicilian olives.

INGREDIENTS

— 50ml London dry gin
— 15ml vermouth
— 10ml olive water
  (page 173)
— 2 green olives, to garnish

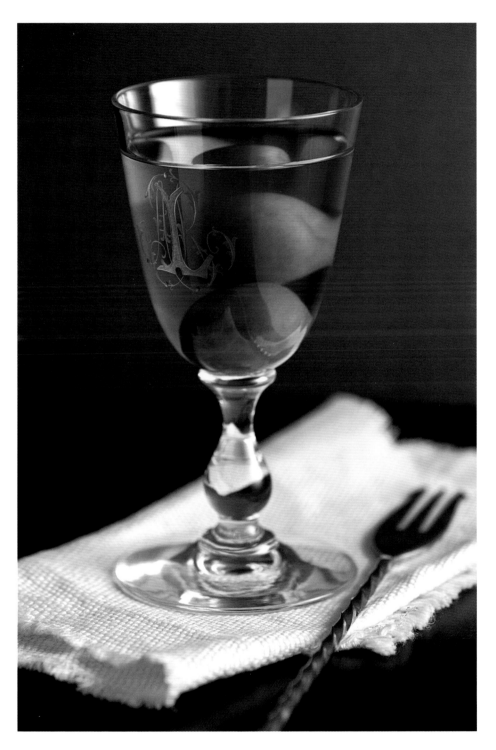

Dirty Martini

Bloody Mary ²⁰¹⁰

This version of the Bloody Mary is all about isolating the components of the cocktail, creating definitive homemade versions and putting them all back together again. I love a good Bloody Mary, and I embarked upon an 18-month clean-up job that removed all the elements I found to be holding back the drink and enhanced all the best bits.

My pet hate in a Bloody Mary is the bitty, gritty texture often produced from including horseradish and pepper granules. I started by re-distilling vodka with fresh horseradish using the Rotavapor in order to retain a punchy kick but without the grainy texture. The resulting vodka is pungent and delicious and really shines through the tomato juice, invoking memories of Sunday lunch. People love the stuff, and I often get requests to sell bottles of it to vodka enthusiasts! The pepper granules that are normally ground over the Bloody Mary are replaced by a pepper distillate that integrates perfectly when stirred into the drink. I'm always dissatisfied with the fermented off-note that comes from using Tabasco and so I make a hot pepper sauce that retains the slight woodiness of chilli along with a real, clean bite of pepper.

Most tomato juices you can find in the supermarket are watery, a dissatisfying result that can also come from fresh-pressing tomatoes. To remedy this problem I mixed equal amounts of non-concentrated tomato juice and passata for a gratifying tomato taste and consistency. The miso added to the juice provides an umami (savoury) quality that really fills the mouth, bolstering the entire drink. It makes sure that the heavier, basier notes also stand their ground alongside the high-hitting sharp notes of the horseradish and pepper distillate.

The result is a drink with distinguished components: a clean-tasting Bloody Mary whose flavours hit you at full force but in a linear fashion. Comforting, yet re-energising!

INGREDIENTS

— 50ml homemade horseradish vodka (page 175)
— 15ml fresh lemon juice
— 15ml Worcester sauce
— Pinch of celery salt
— 3 drops of pepper tincture (page 186)
— 3 dashes of hot pepper sauce (page 206)
— 100ml tomato mix (page 165)
— Lemon slice, to garnish

1. Build the ingredients over cubed ice in a highball glass. Beginning with the horseradish vodka, lemon juice and Worcester sauce and finish with the salt and pepper tincture, hot pepper sauce and finally the tomato mix.

2. Stir and add a lemon slice to garnish.

Bloody Mary

FIGURE 3: Bloody Mary – Flavour and Aroma Journey

Vodka

Celery Salt

Black Pepper

4.
INSPIRED BY PERFUME

Inspired by Perfume

I find perfume totally fascinating. It possesses a unique multifaceted nature; perfume can be art, alchemy and commerce – often all at the same time. Reading books on perfumery began as a hobby, sparked by the seductive mix of romanticism and pragmatism inherent to its art. Perfumery is a profession that relies on absolute accuracy, and elements of this can be taken over to cocktails, where making things very precise is essential – simply changing a micron (1000th of a gram) of an ingredient can make an enormous difference. Our sense of smell is responsible for much of our taste experience, meaning that aroma is a key factor to consider when combining flavours.

The effect of scent on mood and ambience has been well documented over the past 10 years. As medicine and psychological techniques have become more advanced, so has our understanding of how the brain interprets odour. I love how, when we smell, the emotion is direct – a message is sent straight to the limbic system of the brain. Books by Mandy Aftel and Luca Turin demonstrate how the working of your nose is interlinked with the way in which flavour works. It is no surprise then that a great perfume has the power to awaken emotions, unearth lost memories and create both an individual and shared nostalgia.

Alchemy is very much like an extended history of alcohol and its production, explaining the preservation of ingredients, flavours and aromas. The act of the alchemist in the workings of perfumery can parallel the bartender in the balancing of a cocktail. They both share the search for the perfect combination, and there are considerable links between flavours and chemicals and how they work together. Combining this knowledge with lengthy internet research, looking at the chemical structures of ingredients used in cocktail making, I realised the extent of the links between the three disciplines and their shared history. This was of an era before food pairing, and chemical analysis was not readily available, so it was a real learning process.

During this time, Audrey Saunders and I sparked a 10-year dialogue (what we refer to as our linguistic ping-pong across the Atlantic), much of which concerned our mutual passion for aroma. We would lament to one another how aroma is so often overlooked. Audrey made a very poignant comparison with the culinary experience: when we're cooking a stew, the heat releases the aroma of the meat and spices and accordingly the finished dish appeals to all of our senses. However, within the cocktail domain, save for hot toddies, we rarely use heat to release flavour. For the most part we chill our cocktails with ice, and when you put a cooling temperature on something it keeps the aroma within. I wanted to find a way to reawaken the potential of aroma in cocktails but without relying on heat. This chapter explores my foray into the world of the perfumer…

A great perfume has the power to awaken emotions, unearth lost memories and create both an individual and shared nostalgia.

Blush ²⁰⁰⁶

A turnaround drink for me, Blush was the first cocktail
I created that harmonised years of studying alchemy,
perfumery and cocktail history. I had always admired the
Hermès perfume house, who often blend rhubarb, grapefruit
and rose to form the central structure to their fragrances.
These ingredients could be found or replicated into food-
grade essences to make the transition into a cocktail. I added
a rose hydrosol to vodka to replicate the taste and aroma of
roses, and set about making a homemade rhubarb cordial
that would capture the freshness of English rhubarb. I then
had to decide which delivery system to use in the cocktail.
Rose, rhubarb and grapefruit share a chemical combination,
and in a lightning-bolt moment of clarity, I realised that
all three ingredients could be both complemented and
amplified by the addition of champagne.

Champagne is served at a slightly higher temperature than
cocktails or spirits, which means that the volatiles carry well
and the bubbles help by propelling the essences to the top of
the drink, consequently magnifying the flavour. On paper,
the Blush suggests sweetness, but the champagne elongates
the flavours by drying them out. The grapefruit zest adds
an incredible effervescence and the flavours and aromas
bleed into one another so that, when drinking, you can't tell
where one flavour begins and another ends.

The name 'Blush' was initially inspired by the blush of a
rose, but I also like the connotations: it is suggestive both
of an emotional shyness and the blossoming of a rosebud.
In this way we can imagine the flavours of the drink being
teased out and slowly opening up. The languid, relaxed
atmosphere of bars can often promote a certain naughtiness,
which begins internally and slowly makes its way to the
surface, imbuing cheeks with a pink glow. Or perhaps
someone has said something salacious and been caught out.

1. Combine the rose vodka, rhubarb cordial and Peychaud's
Bitters over cubed ice in a cocktail tin and stir.

2. Strain into a chilled coupette or flute. Add the
champagne and a grapefruit twist.

INGREDIENTS
— 25ml rose vodka
   (page 181)
— 15ml rhubarb cordial
   (page 168)
— 2 dashes of
   Peychaud's Bitters
— 75ml champagne
— Grapefruit twist
   (page 221), to finish

Blush

Lipstick Rose ²⁰⁰⁷

I have always been a huge fan of the perfumer Ralf Schwieger for his incredibly conceptual work. Schwieger collaborated with Yves Saint Laurent on his Baby Doll perfume and later for Frederic Malle, with whom he created the Lipstick Rose, and from which this cocktail takes its inspiration.

The Lipstick Rose is named for 1940s femmes fatales, pin-ups and movie icons, whose images are synonymous with their bold red lipsticks. The lipstick of this generation bears little resemblance to the glosses of modern day; they are thick, matte lipsticks with the distinct aroma of violets. For me, these are the women who epitomise the cocktail-drinking glamour generation – delivering sassy one-liners before leaving behind only a lipstick imprint on a champagne glass and a waft of their perfume as they saunter off to break another heart. In this way, the Lipstick Rose is an ode to pure attitude.

I didn't want to create a literal translation of the perfume, but rather transcribe the images that are evoked by its scent. This proved far more complex than other perfume-inspired cocktails I had worked on. I had to break down the components that made up the lipstick aroma. I wanted the cocktail to smell as if the perfume were being drunk, yet allowing the drink to have a floral, fruity taste all of its own. I therefore had to create a new balance of the notes directly present in the perfume to translate it into the cocktail format.

I distilled rose petals into a hydrosol (a water-based essence that suspends essential oils inside water) and achieved a raspberry note by using a syrup for a fresh, rather than stewed, note. It was a long search for a violet flavour that was natural and beautiful but I eventually found a food-grade essence that executed this perfectly. Finally, the zest of grapefruit provided the aroma and oiliness of the perfume's namesake lipstick.

INGREDIENTS
— 15ml rose vodka (page 181)
— 5ml raspberry and violet syrup (page 180)
— Dash of Peychaud's Bitters
— 100ml champagne
— Grapefruit twist (page 221), to garnish
— Homemade lipstick (page 212)

Continues overleaf

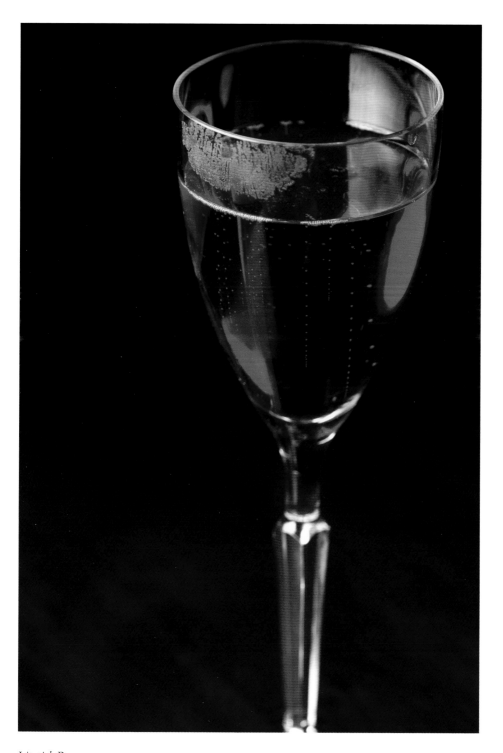

Lipstick Rose

I had a rubber stamp made to emulate a full-mouthed pout and this is pressed into homemade lipstick and imprinted onto the side of the glass. The homemade lipstick is made from carnauba, a natural wax present in most lipsticks and mixed with food-grade essences that match the violet, rose and raspberry flavours of the cocktail. The lipstick kiss works as a multifunctional garnish. It seems counter-intuitive to drink through a lipstick mark, but in addition to being a humorous talking point, the lipstick really enhances the flavours of the drink and the oiliness of the wax mirrors the grapefruit oils that float on top the cocktail. I really like how this drink functions as a total reversal of what a customer expects from a cocktail.

1. Using a lips-shaped rubber stamp, imprint the lipstick kiss along the rim of a champagne flute or coupette.

2. Pour the rose vodka and raspberry and violet syrup directly into the glass, adding a dash of Peychaud's Bitters.

3. Top with the champagne and stir slightly. Finish with a twist of the grapefruit zest and discard.

Gonzales ²⁰¹⁰

Some cocktail ideas are born simply from the drinking habits of friends. My friend Jennifer loved to drink tequila but over the years I'd become bored with always making her margaritas. The idea behind the Gonzales was to move away from marrying tequila with lime and rather to emphasise the honey and caramel notes found in a reposado tequila. The cocktail originally bore the grand name Armando Torres Gonzales, as the first time Jennifer tried it she claimed it to be reminiscent of her first, sweet-smelling, Mexican lover.

I wanted to use two sweet ingredients that would excite but not overpower the other tequila flavours. I combined mineral water and leatherwood honey to marry woody, earthy notes with a salted caramel liqueur. The honey and caramel float with the lemon – they are complex flavours that complement each other and push each other upwards. After visiting Mexico and learning more about the agave plant, and later a study of perfumery, I was able to manipulate this knowledge to really understand and therefore amplify the flavours of this drink. This is how tuberose hydrosol became a late addition to the mix.

A hydrosol is a water-based essence that suspends essential oils inside water, and is an essential ingredient in perfume-making because it is an extremely useful way to deliver delicate flavour. An efficient method of making a hydrosol is by using a Büchi rotary evaporator (a Rotavapor). The Rotavapor (see page 160) allows distillation to take place but under a vacuum, so that you are able to change the boiling temperature. This means that delicate ingredients, whose volatiles would normally be destroyed at boiling temperature, can be released.

INGREDIENTS

— 40ml reposado tequila
— 10ml salted caramel liqueur (page 183)
— 5ml tuberose honey water (page 172)
— Lemon twist (page 221), to garnish

Continues overleaf

Tuberose is a relation of the agave plant, from which tequila is made. The pure essence of tuberose is literally worth its weight in gold, and is traditionally used in perfume. It has an incredible, sweet, floral scent, somewhat similar to honey but with spicy undertones. Using a tuberose hydrosol transformed the Gonzales into a cocktail with incredible depth and seamless layers. Complex, yet drinkable, this is a cocktail that has appealed equally to tequila connoisseurs and those with a more hesitant attitude towards the Mexican spirit.

1. Combine all the ingredients except the lemon over cubed ice in a cocktail tin and stir.

2. Strain into a small, chilled coupette and finish with a small lemon twist.

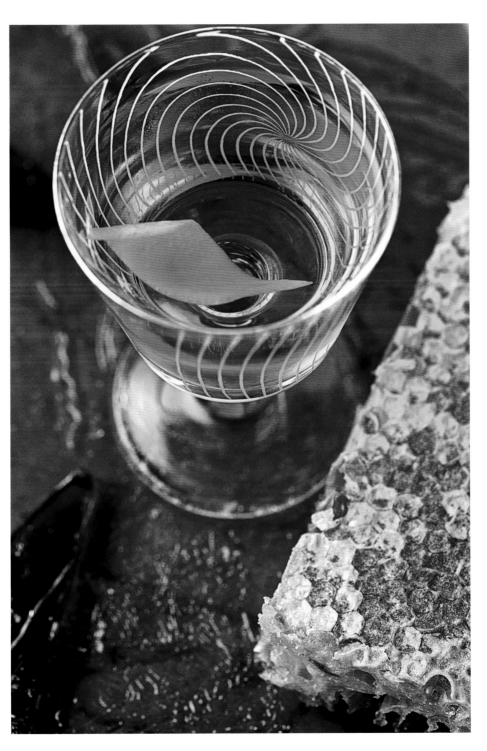

Gonzales

The Rose ²⁰¹⁰

For the next step in my perfumery project, I wanted to create a blend of aromas that would result in a unique signature scent, rather than replicating an already established perfume. The concept for The Rose was simple: I wanted to recreate the experience of sipping a glass of champagne while walking through an English summer garden. I already knew that rose and champagne worked well together, and I built the other ingredients around this basic structure in order to amplify the depth of the bloom. The champagne couldn't be too heavy – the notes had to be allowed to come through. I talked to my sommelier friend Kelvin who suggested that Perrier-Jouët with its delicate, rosy, musky notes would be a perfect match.

In classical perfumery there are three layers of notes that evaporate at different times once the fragrance has been sprayed. When a perfume lands on skin, the first notes to reach your nose are the delicate and volatile top notes. These top notes consist of small and light molecules. The deeper, more mellow middle notes emerge as the top notes dissipate. The base notes are rich and deep and lingering. I took this perfume pyramid as the structure for how the cocktail would work.

The Rose is all about precision. The food-grade essences are extremely strong and so need to be measured in microns using a pipette (see page 158). The essences are mixed with alcohol and put on a sugar cube cut to exactly the same size every time the cocktail is made. The sugar cube aggravates the bubbles, resulting in a surge that propels the aroma right through the cocktail. The carbon dioxide carries and amplifies the aroma and flavour, and as the bubbles split, they release a jet of flavour.

The alcohol works to dissipate the aroma oils by pulling them apart and spreading the aroma, which has previously been trapped in the oil. An ordinary champagne flute traps the aroma and so I use a teardrop flute that holds 100ml of liquid. In this way, the bouquet of the rose opens up, and the three tiers of notes replicate the journey of its bloom.

INGREDIENTS
— 1 white La Perruche sugar cube
— 10 microns of rose essence
— 100ml Perrier-Jouët

As this cocktail is drunk, an incredible sensory loop develops: aroma follows taste, follows aroma, follows taste, becoming fuller and richer with each sip.

1. Prepare a sugar cube by soaking it in 10 microns of rose essence, added to it with a pipette.

2. Place the soaked sugar cube in a Riedel grappa glass and top with champagne.

The Rose

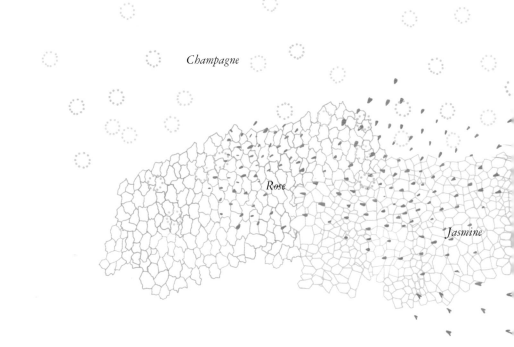

Champagne

Rose

Jasmine

Figure 4: The Rose – Flavour and Aroma Journey

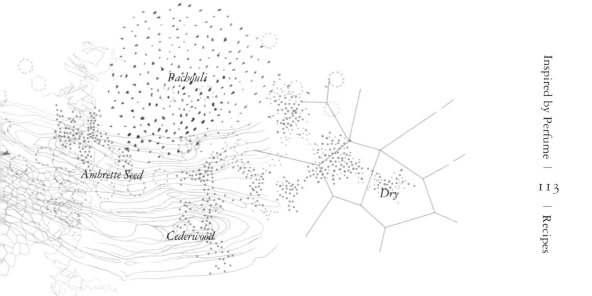

Patchouli

Ambrette Seed

Cederwood

Dry

Koln Martini ²⁰¹¹

Inspired by a cologne recipe found in the second edition of Jerry Thomas' *Bartender's Guide*, the Koln Martini re-figures and modernises the marriage of perfumery and cocktails by using food-grade essences to create a multi-layered spritz. Thomas was the first to galvanise the link between these two crafts. The 1887 edition of his manual showcases how, just as chefs have the ability to work with spice in dry form, bartenders are able to do the same in liquid. In fact, Thomas pioneered the idea of a liquid spice rack by making simple macerations of herbs and spices in alcohol.

With the benefit of technological advances since Thomas's day, the Koln Martini is one of the few perfume drinks I've created that doesn't employ champagne to deliver aroma. The tincture combines petit grain (the distillate of leaves and twigs of the citrus fruit), with vetiver African grass, which produces a salty, green, musky quality. This combination seeks to directly link aroma with the flavours and molecules in gin by identifying and then stripping away its layers. As the notes evaporate at different times they attach themselves to the individual flavours of the gin.

The way in which we taste depends on each molecule's different rate of evaporation. This is dictated by how the molecules are bonded together and consequently how those bonds fall apart. The looser bonds are the ones we taste first, just as in aroma the lightest notes are inhaled first. Each layer of citrus peels off as the drink is consumed. The aroma is ethereal: big on the nose at first but disappearing quickly and playing gently upon the palate. There is, however, real depth to each layer. Using a pipette to deliver the tincture is for both practical and aesthetic reasons. Adding the tincture at the table or bar ensures that the impact of flavour is fresh but also provides an element of theatre and a reference to the more rudimentary practices of perfumery.

1. Combine the gin and vermouth in a cocktail tin and stir over cubed ice.

2. Strain into a goblet and add two drops of the Koln tincture. Finish with a cleaned lemon leaf.

INGREDIENTS
— London Dry gin
— 10ml dry vermouth
— 2 pipette drops of Koln aromatics (page 190)
— Cleaned lemon leaf, to garnish

Koln Martini

5.
CONCEPT DRINKS

Introduction _____

Concept Drinks

The term 'concept drink' is a tricky one. It implies a sense of the absurd rather than abstract, of drama as opposed to discreet theatre. For me, drinks that have arisen from abstract concepts provide an endlessly interesting way to blur the lines between the craft of bartending, philosophy, art and science.

What is a bartender doing in a science lab? That is a question I'm asked all the time. My response is always the same: I love to break boundaries! Over the years I have found that the best way to do this is to research – and then utilise – disciplines and methodologies outside the parameters of bartending. Modern bartending is about crafting drinks by stepping out into the world around us, not being limited by the perceived borders of any one profession. This mantra has meant that one of the most important parts of my working life, and perhaps also the most unusual, is the technology and science used every day at the Drink Factory laboratory.

Ten years of research, borrowing, blagging and buying have resulted in the lab being full of equipment that most would usually associate with chefs, and even hospitals! My relationship with the first-acquired piece of equipment, the Rotavapor (used to distil a solvent or extract delicate flavours, see page 160), is indicative of my approach to using chemistry to create cocktails. I first saw the Rotavapor used in dessert-making by Jordi Roca in Spain and I was transfixed by its accuracy and consistency during the cooking process. The Fat Duck later let me use their Rotavapor and I went wild, putting everything I could through the machine. I spent a long time seeing what I could do with it, exploring its limits. I had to get one for myself! I bought a Rotavapor and it lived in my kitchen for a long time. I quickly learnt to record everything – with delicate machinery every nuance makes an incredible difference to the final distillation.

I spent a long time refining processes and methodologies, straying from the manuals and technical brochures, documenting a way to suit working with cocktails. For instance, I often found that an unbalanced result from the Rotavapor created a product that worked really well in cocktails. In fact, I now purposely misuse a lot of my lab equipment.

Eventually my collection of equipment outgrew the kitchen, then outgrew the space upstairs at my bar at 69 Colebrooke Row, and is now comfortably housed in a fully functioning laboratory nearby. I'm indebted to the lab because it allows me to make a product exactly how I want it, so that I don't have to work constrained by other people's ideas of flavour. It also doesn't have to be complicated: sometimes it's as simple as using a bain-marie rather than spending time hovering over a pan. Equally important is that I can replicate recipes over and over again with incredible accuracy. Consistency is the linchpin of good bartending but it also helps with the logistics of running a bar – making a business work without compromising creativity. With a functioning lab, all ingredients are freshly made, polished and bespoke to our needs.

This profession has afforded me the opportunity to travel extensively and each time I have visited or revisited a country, I've been able to learn more about philosophies and methodologies that I might not otherwise have encountered. Nearly all of my drinks begin life drawn as a flow chart with signifiers of the initial idea behind the drink, flavour combinations and possible ingredients. As this chapter explores, concept drinks do not, therefore, pivot purely upon technology but are about inspiration, developing a snippet of philosophy or a lingering line of poetry and translating this into something delicious.

Cocktails are about little moments of time; each drink has a reference point that sparked its creation, and from this a narrative develops. So then you have to figure out how you make science and emotion work together. As this chapter explores, I've found that science can provide the rationale to help release the emotive element of a drink.

Camomile Cooler ²⁰⁰⁶

The Camomile Cooler was the first drink I ever made using a foam and it remains a favourite to this day. The bottom of the drink is drunk through the foam to release a refreshing hit of both flavours. The cocktail is essentially a whisky sour with a camomile foam, yet it really gets people talking and changes their expectations of what a cocktail experience can be.

1. Combine all the ingredients except the foam in a cocktail tin and stir over cubed ice.

2. Shake and then strain into a rocks glass.

3. Top with camomile foam.

INGREDIENTS

— 50ml Scotch whisky
— 25ml fresh lemon juice
— 15ml sugar syrup
— Camomile foam
  (page 195)

Camomile Cooler

Prairie Oyster ²⁰⁰⁷

In the film *Cabaret*, Liza Minnelli's character Sally Bowles starts every day with a Prairie Oyster – a spiced, raw egg yolk in brandy, consumed as a hair of the dog. I blended this idea with that classic hangover cure the Bloody Mary to create a concoction that sits in taste, texture and aesthetics right on the boundary between food and drink.

I spent a long time deconstructing the Prairie Oyster recipe to separate out the flavours, seeking a way to make a clear distinction between each individual component. I adopted a technique that they invented at El Bulli to create a yolk that has a liquid centre and a gelatine casing. The tomato juice is frozen in a small round mould, shaped just like a natural egg yolk and this is dipped in gelatine. The gelatine creates a tomato 'yolk' that bursts in your mouth. The finely chopped shallots and Kigo shochu mix reference the traditional method of serving oysters.

Serving the cocktail in an oyster shell means that the drink has to be slurped, not sipped, thereby altering your perception of taste and texture. The idea behind this is to change the way the drink is tasted simply by its method of ingestion. By slurping, you pull more air into your mouth, inhaling more oxygen and aerating the flavour, thereby tasting it with your sense of smell. You get an initial hit of pepper sauce, shallots and Kigo and when the tomato yolk bursts it releases a clean, vivid, cherry tomato flavour. This counteracts the intensity of the other flavours but then unifies them so that they are wholly refreshing. Using Kigo rather than the more traditional vodka provides the Prairie Oyster with umami – a long-lasting, mouth-watering taste that really fills the mouth.

This recipe takes time but is less complicated than it seems and is a real showstopper. It provides an incredibly different perspective on how a drink can be both consumed and appreciated, blurring the boundaries between food and liquid.

INGREDIENTS
— 400g cherry tomatoes
— 0.01g MSK orange food dye
— 1g vege-gel
— 1g soya lecithin
— 290ml Worcester sauce
— 25ml Kigo shochu
— Dash of raspberry vinegar
— Dash of olive oil
— 5ml fresh lemon juice
— Dash of hot pepper sauce (page 206)
— Pinch of finely chopped shallots
— Pinch of celery salt
— Pinch of black pepper

1. To make the tomato juice, slice a tiny incision into the skin of each tomato using a sharp knife. Place the tomatoes in a jug, pour boiling water over them and leave for 5 minutes before draining. Peel off any remaining skin with your fingers, and blitz the tomatoes with a hand blender. Push the mush through a sieve then through a centrifuge, which will clarify the liquid. Add the orange food dye.

2. Pour the tomato juice into a silicone half-sphere mould and freeze overnight. Carefully remove the frozen yolks from the mould.

3. Put the vege-gel in a pan with 500ml of water, heat the solution to 80°C and then allow to cool to 55°C. Check the temperature regularly and if it drops below 45°C, reheat to 80°C and start again.

4. Using a long pin, spike the frozen tomato 'yolks' and dip them into the vege-gel twice. It will set instantly, forming a skin around the shape. Place each yolk on greaseproof paper, and when you have completed the required amount, place them all in the freezer and leave for approximately one hour. As the yolks defrost they become clearer in colour and the ice is visibly melted inside. When the centre of the yolks are liquid, they are ready to use.

5. Combine the soya lecithin with the Worcester sauce and blitz with a hand blender until a foamy consistency. This will make a light and frothy 'air' to sit on top of the yolk.

6. Combine the Kigo, vinegar, oil, lemon juice, hot pepper sauce and shallots in a mixing bowl and stir. Place each egg yolk in an oyster shell and then spoon the Kigo mix over the top, followed by the Worcester 'air'. Season with celery salt and pepper.

Pictured overleaf

Prairie Oyster

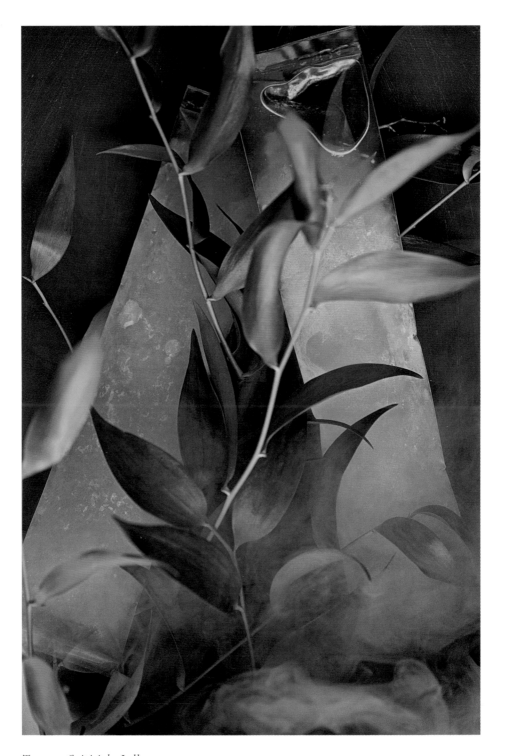

Tarragon Caipirinha Lolly

Tarragon Caipirinha Lolly [2008]

In life there are party drinks – sugar-loaded syrupy cocktails – and there are drinks that are made for partying. The Tarragon Caipirinha Lolly falls into the latter category and was designed as a fun solution to that tiresome problem of dancing and holding your drink at the same time.

Originally made for a cachaça brand in time for a Brazilian-style festival in London, this drink takes a classic caipirinha and subverts it by subtly enhancing the flavour of the sugar cane and using tarragon to produce a cold, tingly sensation on the tongue, which also imbues the mix with a beautiful light-green colour. The lollipop style is the perfect accompaniment to some grown-up fun…

1. Combine all the ingredients except the dry ice in a large mixing bowl. Stir vigorously.

2. Pour into lolly bags and seal with a vacuum or a ziplock bag. Freeze in dry ice, if possible, or in a freezer if not available.

INGREDIENTS

— 1g tarragon juice
  (page 163)
— 700ml cachaça
— 350ml clear lime
  (page 165)
— 175ml sugar cane syrup
— 1 litre mineral water
— Dry ice, for freezing

Cosmo Popcorn ²⁰⁰⁵

Many great food innovations have been discovered entirely by mistake and this delicious twist on the Cosmopolitan is no exception. Whilst at The Fat Duck's experimental lab, their pastry chef Jockey and I were trying to create a Bellini macaroon by combining a foam with liquid nitrogen. The result was an interesting hard/soft texture but it didn't quite work for a Bellini. Instead, we created a cranberry-heavy Cosmopolitan and, using a siphon, sprayed it as foam on top of liquid nitrogen. Alarmingly, the frozen foam started to crack and make a popping sound. Eventually it shattered and we scooped out the remains with a spoon. The foam had kernelled and the result looked just like pieces of popcorn. Each bite delivered an incredible cold crunch alongside direct flavour that turned to liquid in the mouth. Since there was no dilution, the full, instantly recognisable flavour of the Cosmopolitan hit you. We made wax paper cones and scooped the Cosmo Popcorn into them, along with plastic ice-cream spoons to devour them with.

The science behind this novelty drink unfortunately results in an utter impracticability for service at a bar. Use of liquid nitrogen should be confined only to the professional kitchen.

1. Add the gelatine sheets to the cranberry juice and heat in a pan until 80°C and the gelatine has completely dissolved. Remove from the heat and wait until cool, then combine all the ingredients and place them in an ISI siphon.

2. Charge the siphon with two N2O cartridges and place in the fridge to cool for an hour.

3. Pour some of the liquid nitrogen into a large, stainless-steel, insulated bowl. Remove the siphon from the fridge and, from a safe distance, squirt the cosmo mix at regular intervals into the bowl of liquid nitrogen. Use a wire-mesh ladle to scoop the popcorn out of the stainless-steel bowl. Repeat with more liquid nitrogen and more of the mix.

4. Scoop into paper ice-cream cones and serve with a flat plastic ice-cream spoon.

INGREDIENTS
— 2 gelatine sheets
— 200ml cranberry juice
— 100ml vodka
— 75ml triple sec
— 75ml egg white
— 20ml fresh lime juice
— 20ml lime cordial
  (page 167)
— 10ml orange bitters
— 50ml sugar syrup

FOR THE SERVE
— Paper ice-cream cones
  and plastic ice-cream
  spoons

Cosmo Popcorn

Triple Sec

Sugar

Citrus Vodka

Cranberry

FIGURE 5: Cosmo Popcorn – Flavour and Aroma Journey

Nitrogen

Egg White

Lime Cordial

Water

Water

Haiku

Haiku [2009]

The Haiku is all about discreet theatre. Influenced by the Japanese notion of working with the seasons, this cocktail is evocative of sitting beneath a cherry blossom tree and was created as a means of demonstrating the idea that however something falls, it falls...

The three ingredients used in the Haiku reflect the different components of shochu. Rice water is delicate and incredibly drinkable and makes a direct link to the rice used in the making of shochu. The almond milk draws out the almond notes in Kigo, and the cedar wood also present in the rice milk provides a depth and woodiness that reinforces the concept of whiling away an afternoon languishing beneath a cherry blossom tree.

1. Combine the almond rice water and shochu in a cocktail tin and stir over cubed ice.

2. Strain into a small, chilled coupette and serve next to a ramekin of scented cherry-blossom rice paper to be scattered over the finished drink.

Rice Paper Garnish

1. To flavour the rice paper, soak one ball of cotton wool with cherry-blossom essence and cherry-blossom wood essence (both food-grade) and place at the bottom of a jam-jar. Cover the cotton with a mesh wire, and sit the rice paper on top.

2. Suspend a muslin bag full of dry rice over the top and seal the jar, allowing the rice paper to absorb the aroma.

3. Leave for at least 2 days, or up to 1 week.

INGREDIENTS
— 20ml almond milk rice water (page 171)
— 40ml Kigo shochu
— White-tea-scented cherry-blossom rice paper (see below)

The Morning After the Night Before ²⁰¹⁰

Makes 4 200ml bottles

This drink is inspired by the morning-after ritual of reaching for a glass of water and a tablet to relieve the pain incurred from the previous evening… It's served in a bottle with a tablet on the side, which, when dropped into the glass, carbonates the drink with a dramatic rush of bubbles powering up from the bottom. The concept here is one of action, expectation and anticipation; when we crack open a can of soda, part of the enjoyment is pulling the ring and hearing the sound of the fizz. This ritual sets up our expectation for the drink.

The drink is reminiscent of a classic Gin Fizz but has been made clear and still. As the bottle is opened there is a disappointing lack of fizz, which goes hand in hand with that deflated morning-after feeling. The 'fizz' is found in the tablet sitting alongside the bottle. When the tablet is dropped into the gin it reacts and bubbles, raising the spirits and inspiring a hope for relief from the morning's pains…

1. Mix the water, gin, lemon and sugar syrup in a jug and separate the mix into four bottles.

2. Serve a soda tablet beside each bottle.

INGREDIENTS
— 400ml still mineral water
— 250ml gin
— 125ml clear lemon (page 164)
— 75ml sugar syrup
— 2g bicarbonate of soda tablet, to serve

The Morning After the Night Before

Silver Mountain ²⁰¹⁰

One of the perks of working in the bartending world is being given the opportunity to travel. Whilst designing the menu for the Shochu Lounge, I went back and forth to Japan researching flavours and techniques. In particular I loved picking up some of the soft drinks and types of shochu that weren't available for export. The beautiful six-generation Kyo-ya distillery in Nichinan, Kyushu, became a subject of fascination for me and I visited it many times, building a relationship with the master distiller. It was here that I fell in love with the soft and delicate Kigo.

Dave Broom, friend and spirits expert, once tasted Kigo and remarked that it was like exquisite water. This sparked for me a vision of a Japanese woodland stream, reminiscent of the beautiful river that runs down the mountain next to the distillery. I wanted to emulate the taste of really fresh, cold, spring water – a flavour inextricable from the aroma of its woodland surrounding. I always envisage a running stream as a translucent silver colour, implying its movement as it catches the light of the sun or moon; from this image the Silver Mountain was born.

It was never my intention for philosophy to act as the inspiration behind this drink but it bled its way into all the parameters of a cocktail with such a specific concept. In this way, the image of a silver mountain came first and I built the ingredients around it accordingly. One of the things I like most about Japanese culture and cuisine is the inextricable link between the two. Japanese cooking reflects the natural environment that surrounds it and is quintessentially seasonal. The minimalism of this drink is an intentional reflection of the element of subtraction in Japanese cooking; the best is drawn from what nature gives us, what is unnecessary is removed and what is most desired is accentuated.

INGREDIENTS
— 50ml Kigo shochu
— 25ml Silver Needle tea (page 172)
— 2.5ml sugar
— 2 Ruscus leaves, to garnish

Shochu is traditionally drunk with green tea and I wanted to create a bridge between its traditional serve and my woodland concept. The Japanese tea ceremony is a cultural activity involving the ceremonial preparation and presentation of matcha, which is powdered green tea. The tea is made in a minimally adorned room whilst a poem is read; the room is understated but indicates greater signifiers outside the room. These include an aesthetic of humility, restraint and simplicity. In this way, the formalities of the ceremony are full of implied meaning. With this in mind, I wanted to create a cocktail that built upon an understated minimalism existing within the framework of a big concept.

I began by working with green tea but found it too overpowering an ingredient for the cocktail format. I liked the idea of jasmine growing by the side of the stream, but again the flavour became more about the tea than the Kigo. It was at this point that I experimented with Silver Needle tea, which is delicate and has a soft quality to it. I brewed the tea at exactly 70°C and let it steep for 5 minutes. Every tea has its optimum brewing point, and it is important not to use boiling water since it can destroy some of the tea's flavour.

To replicate the earthy, woody and slightly vegetable aroma of a mountain stream I used cassis leaf, which has a gentle sulphur note to it reminiscent of bark, with a 'just rained' green scent. This particular sulphur quality reminded me of stones found in and around streams. After playing around with adding sugar, I finally settled on a very minimal use. Its purpose is not as a sweetener but rather to give a mouth-feel so that it has a substrata flavour and effect; since the brain doesn't record the flavour, you don't notice the sweetness as a taste but it does register the mouth-feel.

For the garnish, I used Ruscus leaves to imitate the way that leaves fall into a river and are swept along by the running water. As it passes you, a stream gives you a photograph of an instant, of which you only catch one piece. In this way I could imply a sense of history of where the stream has been and where it is going...

1. Combine all the ingredients except the Ruscus leaves in a cocktail tin and stir over cubed ice.

2. Strain and pour into a large, chilled coupette and garnish with two Ruscus leaves.

Plume ²⁰¹⁰

The Plume alludes to elements of the traditional Japanese tea ceremony, aiming to create a sense of space through ritual. There are four principles of the Japanese ceremony: harmony, respect, purity and tranquillity. This drink makes reference to purity – to be cleansed through the senses. The pea shoot appeals to the sense of sight, sense of touch comes into play when we handle the utensils, sense of smell when we inhale the incense, and sense of taste when drinking the cocktail.

At a Japanese incense 'smelling ceremony' I learnt a lot about making incense by talking to those who make it professionally. Making my own incense turned into a far nicer project than I'd anticipated – it was very tactile. I'd make a paste of the chosen ingredients with water and then dry it out with a hydrator. Working with dry aromas rather than liquid ones was a totally new experience for me.

For me, delivering aroma via incense was particularly interesting. The incense is utilised as a way of enhancing flavour in addition to creating a meditative mood. I like the way the idea of aroma is reversed – delivered not inside the drink itself but around it. To create the incense, I identified a series of elements linking back to the drink and ordered them directly from Japan. Using smoke and thinking about how smoke reacts, as opposed to pure aroma or perfume, means that the drink has a completely different delivery. There's something very calming about watching that small plume of smoke circling the drink.

1. Combine all the ingredients in a cocktail tin and stir over cubed ice. Strain into a thimble glass. Serve as follows.

2. Pour the white sand into a small Japanese metal-enamelled bowl, leaving a 1cm lip, and brush the sand with a fan brush.

3. Place the cut affila sprig, thimble glass and incense in a triangle shape in the sand. Light the incense and serve once it starts to smoke.

INGREDIENTS
— 40ml gin
— 20ml Silver Needle tea
  (see page 172)
— 10ml Kigo shochu

FOR THE SERVE
— Handful of white sand
— 1 green tea incense cone
  (page 210)
— 1 affila sprig (pea shoot)

Plume

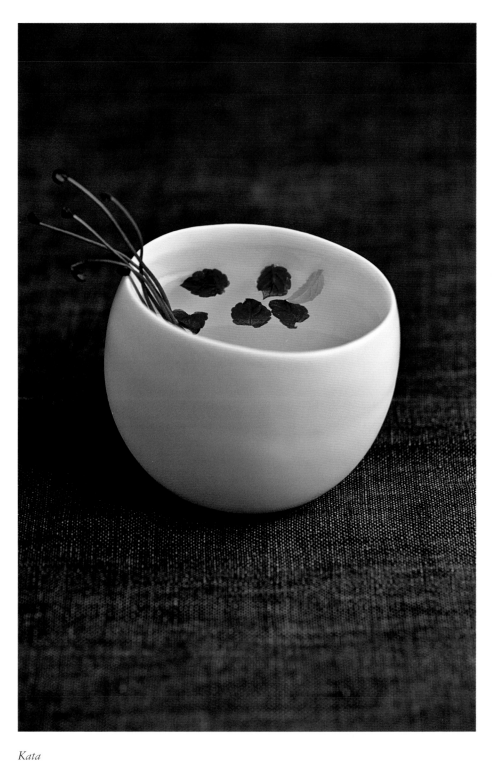

Kata

Kata ²⁰¹⁰

For centuries, Japanese culture has revered nature as an ideal of beauty. Instead of imposing a manmade concept of beauty on the landscape, nature is synthesised in miniature awe-inspiring gardens. I once visited a beautiful restaurant in Ninchen, Japan, where the entire landscape was manicured according to the seasons in a tradition that dated back to the Emperor's gardens in the 1800s. The result is an incredibly structured composition of nature; the garden blooms in total harmony, each plant carefully worked out for its moment of bloom.

The serve of this cocktail is entirely focused on creating a setting using Ikebana – the Japanese art of flower arrangement – as inspiration. In addition to the aesthetic, Ikebana creates harmony by emphasising different parts of the arrangement in a minimal way. It is not considered a flower arrangement but an arrangement with flowers. In the Kata, the chives are reminiscent of reeds peeking out of water.

The Kata pivots on the flavours of basil and shiso – two herbs from the same family but used in different cultures. The basil and shiso overlap within the drink and work together in an interesting flavour fusion to deconstruct the savoury flavours in both the gin and vermouth. The result is herby but delicate, with the slight sweetness of basil playing in the background. Green, aromatic and lush, to coincide with the herbaceous gin, this drink is about an outward harmony as well as a harmony between neatly interlocking ingredients.

1. Combine the basil gin and shiso dry vermouth in a cocktail tin and stir over cubed ice. Strain and pour into a Japanese bone-china sake cup.

2. Garnish with five rock chives bound with a sixth chive like a daisy chain and shiso cress.

INGREDIENTS
— 40ml basil gin
  (page 202)
— 10ml shiso dry vermouth
  (page 203)
— 6 rock chives and shiso
  cress, to garnish

Master at Arms ²⁰¹⁰

Although it is true that cocktails have an impressive 200-year history, most classic cocktails are American in origin and survivors from a very narrow period of time. It can be hard to break free of this traditional frame of reference so I spent a long time researching the Georgian period, wondering what ingredients would be available to the discerning Georgian drinker. Britain has a long history as a colonial and seafaring power and the Master at Arms is a naval rank referring to an officer responsible for physical training and security upon a mercantile ship. He would also often be in charge of doling out rum and port rations. It occurred to me that a stirred-down rum drink would be an elegant companion to a voyage, Georgian or otherwise!

When it comes to rum cocktails it is very easy to reach for the same flavour connections. Eliminating the addition of citrus juice transforms the flavour profile of rum in a cocktail and results in a drink miles apart from the fruity rum cocktails I normally work with. The first combination of rum and port proved too sweet and too strong so I set about making a port reduction in the Rotavapor (page 160) so that I could evaporate the alcohol in a very controlled way. Once the port has gone through the Rotavapor it becomes incredibly light; in this way the port reduction can work in the same spirit-to-sweetener ratio as in El Presidente (page 39) or a Manhattan (page 26). The opulent, ruby red of this drink is somewhat of an illusion as the aroma gives way to a rich fruitiness and a pleasing dryness with a surprisingly long finish.

Light and playful, this drink uses technology to bring it to life. The result is very classic and deceptively simple, but the process used to get there is as modern as it gets.

1. Combine all the ingredients in a cocktail tin and stir over cubed ice.

2. Strain and pour into a small, chilled coupette.

3. Tie a small piece of black rope into a sailor's knot around the stem of the glass to serve.

INGREDIENTS
— 50ml dark rum
— 20ml port reduction (page 176)
— 5ml homemade grenadine (page 182)

FOR THE SERVE
— Black rope, for sailor's knot decoration

Master at Arms

Les Fleurs du Mal

Les Fleurs du Mal ²⁰¹¹

Baudelaire's *Les Fleurs du Mal* ('The Flowers of Evil') was
published in 1857 and immediately caused public outrage
for scaling the terrain of moral corruption, sexual perversion
and alcoholic candour. The volume is a fascinating study of
fragrance, intimacy and ravishing beauty that can be fuelled
by sin or exist side by side with darkness. Re-reading
the poem one afternoon, its discussion of the delicate
dichotomy between beauty and darkness became the
premise for this cocktail.

I love the chequered history of absinthe. Its historical
associations are of a banned, evil and taboo substance and
in France particularly, rouse images of vice. However,
in moderate doses, absinthe was allied with inspiration:
new views, unique feelings and a peculiarly clear form of
intoxication. A million miles away from the seedy taverns
of Paris, absinthe has traditionally been used alongside rose
as an ingredient in perfume. This is primarily to extort
its fragrant anise and wormwood, but also to release more
subtle herbs such as Florence fennel, Melissa, hyssop and
angelica root.

I wanted to avoid the obvious ways of including absinthe
in a cocktail by pairing it with ingredients that were floral,
light and delicate, with the absinthe ominously nestling
beside. Essentially a rose sour with a touch of absinthe,
Les Fleurs du Mal represents the contest between the two
contrasting human impulses towards beauty and darkness.

*There are in every man at all times two simultaneous impulses –
one toward God, the other toward Satan.* (Baudelaire's journal)

1. Combine all the ingredients in a cocktail tin.

2. Dry-shake, add cubed ice and shake again. Strain and
pour into a goblet.

INGREDIENTS
— 50ml rose vodka
  (page 181)
— 25ml fresh lemon juice
— 25ml egg white
— 5ml absinthe

Rotavapor

6.

EQUIPMENT & TECHNIQUES

Introduction ─────────────────────── ●

Equipment and Techniques

The equipment housed in my Drink Factory laboratory has been acquired over an eight-year period. During this time, I have not only learnt how to use the equipment to obtain incredibly high levels of accuracy but have also invented techniques that manipulate the abilities of each piece of kit to work uniquely with liquids. This chapter, rather than functioning as a manual, as such, explains how I first came to use each piece of equipment and the methods needed for them to work with the liquid format.

Cooking Sous Vide: the Bain-marie & Vacuum Machine

Cooking 'sous vide' has been a quiet part of the culinary world for years but recently its notoriety has begun to snowball, becoming a catalyst for the scientific revolution in the cooking world over the last five years. Bruno Goussault is both a scientist and an economist who gave momentum to the established practice of cooking sous vide, and he's not even a chef – I love that.

For years I had been working in bars making my own ingredients by macerating and infusing fruits and essences into alcohol, often litres and litres at a time. In terms of consistency this can be incredibly problematic; combining natural ingredients with alcohol, especially fruit, always results in a certain amount of natural degradation. Most alcohols have 40 per cent ABV and the remaining 60 per cent of water will, over time, affect the flavour of the material. For example, if you put fresh raspberries in gin, eventually a musty flavour will develop as the fruit starts to degrade, tainting the entire batch. The solution to this is cooking sous vide.

Cooking sous vide has two distinct parts: sealing ingredients in a bag in a vacuum machine and then cooking them in a bain-marie, which provides a precise regulation of heat. These two pieces of equipment are a dream team: together you have complete control over your ingredients, extracting flavour in an incredibly precise way with satisfying, flavoursome results. The sous vide bag works as a hermetic seal, keeping in both juices and aroma;

and by cooking in water you get better heat transfer than you would in an oven. Sous vide liquids can be served in drinks immediately, but using this method for batch cooking makes the preparation for the bar, or for a party, really practical.

It's crucial to select the correct water temperature for the bain-marie. Finding the perfect time and temperature to achieve the exact results I want often involves a long series of trial and error. I time all my infusions or macerations and meticulously record them in a log book with their corresponding temperatures.

For those who don't have commercial sous vide equipment, it can be replicated at home using simple kitchen items – see page 151.

Step-by-step sous vide

1. Prepare the ingredients.

2. Vacuum-pack.

3. Set temperature for cooking.

4. Cook for a set time in a bain-marie.

5. Rest or cool.

Bain-marie

I first used a bain-marie at Roka in 2005 and it truly revolutionised the way that I was able to make bespoke ingredients. Water baths, or bain-maries, are thought to have originally been created by an alchemist named Maria the Jewess, and were devised to slowly control a rise in temperature using boiling water. Centuries later, their purpose and function has not really changed.

How it works

1. Place the product into a plastic bag.

2. Vacuum-seal the bag.

3. Release the vacuum.

4. Cook for a set time at a set temperature in the bain-marie.

Continues overleaf

I'm a huge fan of this self-contained method of cooking; carefully controlling a gentle heat slowly releases the flavour, and since there is no oxidisation and nowhere for the flavour to escape to, this preserves the natural, delicate flavours that are easily destroyed through heat. One of the biggest advantages we have in modern water baths is that we are able to regulate the temperature to a very specific degree. This allows you to really get the best from the ingredients, ensuring that even very delicate volatiles, such as flowers, are not destroyed during the cooking process.

In addition, cooking ingredients at a low temperature, for longer, bonds the flavours in a more subtle way. The result is an unparalleled smoothness. The water is rotated so that it is always at a constant temperature. This way the heat reaches every part of the ingredient, gently extracting its flavour. This style of cooking is executed with incredible efficiency and consistency.

Vacuum Machine

The vacuum machine has been used for years to preserve food and liquid and enhance their storage life. By sucking all the air (and therefore oxygen) away from a product, vacuum-packing simultaneously forestalls the two biggest causes of food degradation: direct oxidisation and aerobic microbial growth. Consequently, the technology substantially increases shelf life and therefore is incredibly practical for preparation purposes.

It may seem unnatural to store liquid in a plastic bag but vacuum-sealing protects whatever is inside the bag during the cooking process. In addition to the economic value, because everything stays within the bag there is nowhere for the flavour to escape to. We tend to associate the kitchen with the smell of good cooking, but in the lab even though we cook delicious ingredients sous vide all the time, it only ever smells of whatever perfume I've been tinkering with. This is because all of the aroma from the food becomes trapped in the bag. The final product is full of flavour; it smells fantastic, and the fully humid environment inside the bag eliminates drying, which means it's juicy too.

The vacuum machine is the real linchpin behind the practicability of all the other pieces of equipment I use in the lab. One of the first to use the vacuum machine in a bar, I find it absolutely invaluable for preparing and later storing ingredients until they're needed.

How it works

The ingredients or liquids are placed in plastic bags. These are then laid in the chamber, with their open ends on a sealing bar. After the lid is closed, a powerful vacuum pump evacuates the air. The sealing bar heats up, melting a strip of the bag and bonding it closed. The chamber then returns to atmospheric pressure and unlocks the lid.

1. Fill the bag over a cylinder (a large glass or tin, for example) to make it easier to fill without spilling.

2. Set the vacuum level and sealing times on the machine.

3. Place the bag in the chamber. Laying the bag on a ramp will help prevent it from leaking during the sealing process.

Additional benefits

It's a basic bit of kit but the vacuum machine can also be used to do incredible things that it's not supposed to do. For example, I discovered that I could flavour different fruits, not just by putting liquid alongside them in the bag, but by adding it outside the tray. When I was experimenting with the garnish for the Somerset Sour, I was using a melon baller to scoop apple balls, which are very porous and have lots of air and juice in them. Placing these in a tray with a liquid around it (pectin and grass flavour), without a bag, cause the vacuum to pull the juice and air out of the apple. When you turn the machine off, the chamber re-floods and the air rushes back in, forcing the liquid on the tray into what used to be the air cells in the apple. It works just like squeezing a sponge. This modifies the texture of the fruit, so that it is at once juicer and yet crisper – and a truly fantastic garnish! You can do this with any porous fruit that isn't too fibrous.

Cooking Sous Vide at Home

Sous vide technology is becoming more accessible and more affordable, but all recipes that call for sous vide cooking can be replicated at home. Before I could justify buying a bain-marie for myself, I began experimenting with zip-lock bags in pans with thermometers. Water is a better medium for heat transfer than the air in the oven and a far more precise temperature is

Continues overleaf

reached than could be achieved with a pan on the hob. Although labour intensive, it is a really effective way of getting flavour into alcohol, as well as quicker and more consistent than infusions or macerations.

To re-create a bain-marie at home, all you need is two saucepans, one smaller than the other. Pour water into the larger pan, place the smaller one within the larger one, also filled with water, and heat on the hob. You can regulate and monitor the temperature using a thermometer to make sure that the temperature is constant. Just make sure you fine-strain your final product.

The vacuum machine can also be improvised upon. To re-create a vacuum bag, there are a couple of options. You can either buy a cheap sealing unit, which will do an adequate job, or if you are feeling adventurous you can place a straw into the centre of the bag, wrap a rubber band around the top, and suck the air out of the bag manually. It might sound silly but it will get the job done.

Centrifuge

One of the earliest centrifuges was made by Antoni Pranotti in 1864, which at the time was used to separate milk from fat in the production of dairy products. A centrifuge works on the Sedimentation Principle: it uses centrifugal force to separate parts of a mixture that have different densities. This causes liquids of a medium weight to become sandwiched between the denser, heavier liquids that fall to the bottom of the container and the lighter liquids that remain at the top. Centrifuges have a widespread use but since they can be found in oil, medical and scientific labs, the idea of having a centrifuge behind a functioning bar, or back-of-house in restaurants, is probably something still quite alien to most!

The primary purpose of the Drink Factory's centrifuge is to clarify liquid. Colour molecules in liquid are amongst the largest, and the bigger the molecules are, the harder your saliva needs to work in order to break down flavour. If the colour molecules are removed, a more immediate and deeper flavour comes through. Clarified products tend to have a different mouth-feel from non-clarified products since the elements that usually make them cloudy have been removed. The mouth-feel is lighter and smoother, and consequently the final result is a cleaner taste. For example, clarified rhubarb makes for an incredible cordial; rhubarb is naturally very fibrous so I cook the fruit until soft enough to release its flavour, then centrifuge it to remove the pesky fibres that interfere with its flavour. The resulting juice tastes clean and bright without compromising the delicious sweet–tart combination of the fruit.

In addition to mouth-feel, clarified liquid looks fantastic! Serving up a completely clear tomato juice, for example, is an interesting twist that challenges both aesthetic and taste preconceptions. It was at Isola in 1999 that I first began playing around with the idea of clarifying in order to make a Bloody Mary Martini. The idea was to serve vodka stirred with a totally clear tomato juice, using an ice cube frozen with spices that melted as the drink was stirred. The result was often a complete surprise to the customers – a really striking effect that got people talking.

Before I acquired a centrifuge, to make the clear tomato consommé I would have to cook the tomatoes and gently peel off their skin. The skinless tomatoes would be blitzed, mixed with a agar-agar (a gelatine derived from seaweed) and then hung in muslin in the fridge overnight. Colour molecules are bigger than flavour molecules, so by force of gravity the heavier colour molecules slowly drip through the muslin, leaving behind an incredibly flavourful, but totally clear, tomato consommé. In addition to this taking some time, I found that the flavours and aromas of the fridge crept their way into the tomatoes. Using a centrifuge eliminates the aroma problem and produces a superior and more efficient product in just 10 minutes!

The first centrifuge I played around with was borrowed and lived in my kitchen for six months. I spent a long time tinkering with different speeds and angles (as the angle moves out, the greater the centrifugal force). Such lengthy experimentation had the added bonus of being great for my health as I spent this time drinking endless quantities of fresh, clarified juice! It was a logical step to buy a centrifuge for use at the bar, and I purchased my first one in 2009. It completely revolutionised the way I made juice in a commercial environment – I can now batch-make juice and use the vacuum machine to store the product in the fridge. More efficient, cleaner and producing much less waste than any other option, the centrifuge is imperative to the organisation of my lab. If you make a lot of juices in a bar or restaurant, it will pay for itself very quickly.

Soxhlet Still

In 2005 I was experimenting with extracting flavour from bark and fairly hard spices to use in my own bitters. Since I couldn't afford a vacuum at this time, the Soxhlet still was a great way to try out ideas. This still works using an evaporation loop; it evaporates, condenses and evaporates again for as long as is needed. If I put a harder ingredient through the still, such as star anise, I can siphon the oil off the top using a needle. However, this can be quite a long process, taking up to four hours at a time.

Vacuum distillations are more precise but if you don't have the budget for a Rotavapor then this is a really good way to start doing things. You can add a vacuum to this still but that can make it a little tricky to use.

Büchner Funnel with Vacuum Pump

Looking through scientific equipment catalogues in 2006, I came across the Büchner – a fantastic system for filtration. Used when making macerations or infusions, it produces a cleaner product by filtering out the extraneous bits of a maceration (residue, powder and fibres), essentially arresting the flavour so that it doesn't keep aging or change flavour profile over time. Rather than waiting for these residues to drip through, the force of the pump pushes them; this speeds up the entire process and the resulting product will mellow only marginally. I started by using an aquarium pump attachment to provide the vacuum, but soon moved onto the more powerful vacuum pump, which creates a vacuum faster.

The Büchner funnel is a really simple way to make a cleaner and, most importantly, more stable product.

Getting the best out of the Büchner funnel

1. Put the vacuum hose onto the collection chamber.

2. Place the Büchner funnel into the rubber bung at the top of the collection chamber.

3. The choice of filter paper to insert is important – for bigger flavours you want to get more of the liquid out and so need filter paper with bigger micron filters – smaller particles need smaller papers. Filters come in paper and cellulose.

4. Put the liquid you want filtering into the Büchner funnel and turn the vacuum on – this will suck the liquid through, leaving the residue behind.

Microjuicer

The microjuicer is the king of juicers. Fantastic for juicing really fine ingredients such as lemon grass and ginger, a microjuicer effectively removes all the fibres that get in the way of a clean, refined juice. Attachments to make oil are available so that you can retrieve the oils from whatever you put through. These can then be mixed with water so that you can use them later to make hydrosols or your own essential oils.

Induction Heater

An induction heater works using an electromagnet, through which an alternating current is passed. Gas will always fluctuate, so rather than heating ingredients over a naked flame, we use an induction heater every day in the lab to achieve an even heat distribution with consistent and accurate temperatures. The height of practicability, I've had one of these since about 2004 after I first saw pastry chefs using them. Induction heaters are really useful because you can carry them around; this is great for events when I need a heat source outside of the bar or kitchen as it means I don't have to use a dangerous heat source like gas or electric. It makes the process much smoother.

Cold Smoker & Smoke-Gun

Smoky notes in flavour are complex and give a real depth and a new dimension to whatever they are combined with. The cold smoker is more of a unit as opposed to a machine. It allows you to construct an extension so that by the time the smoke gets into the actual chamber it's completely cool. With the smoke cold, you can put things such as fresh fruit in there and smoke them without altering their structure. I first did this with cherries to garnish a Manhattan; deceptively they appear to be fresh-pitted cherries, but once bitten, a slight smokiness is released and in turn this gives an amazing new angle to a Manhattan.

Smoked syrups, which can introduce an interesting and multifaceted element to any cocktail can be simply made with the help of a smoke gun. First you make a smoked sugar by sealing sugar granules in a zip-lock bag and snaking the tube of the smoke-gun inside. Once the smoke has filled the zip-lock bag, pull the tube out and close the bag until the smoke dissipates and is completely absorbed into the sugar. This smoky sugar can then be used to make a syrup, simply by adding water.

Dehydrator

Essentially, a dehydrator is a basic way to draw out moisture from ingredients. It works by blowing hot air through a system of different tiers – like a giant hairdryer but on a lower heat. The heat source can be adjusted according to how slowly you want dehydration to occur; for example, slow dehydration is necessary for more delicate volatiles, and a by-product of this method is that it also preserves them.

The dehydrator is fantastic for getting the best out of a multitude of more esoteric ingredients, exposing the full range of their flavour profile. When exploring the flavour profile of nettles for the Nettle Gimlet (page 68), for example, I found that although fresh nettles have a minty quality, by dehydrating them I could extrapolate more tannic and tea-like notes from the nettle. So I cut the leaves and spread them evenly across the tiers on a low heat, leaving them for a few hours to dry out whilst occasionally rotating the tiers to get an even dryness. Once brewed for use in the cordial, the flavour from the nettles was incredible!

Acquiring a dehydrator also totally changed the way I could work with garnishes. In 2009, I was working on the first version of The Rose (page 110), which I wanted to garnish with rose petals. The only way I could envisage executing this was to dry out the petals so that they wouldn't shrink and wither. Using the dehydrator meant that I could preserve the delicate petals and later go on to infuse them with a rose tincture so that the aroma of the flower could float up from the glass. In addition to expanding my repertoire of garnishes, the water content of food can often be quite high, so using a dehydrator results in a fantastic, more concentrated flavour. This is particularly useful for making purées for savoury-based cocktails. I've found that drying out tomatoes meant that more 'umami' could be extracted from the fruit and this resulted in a richer flavour that could then be used in a homemade passata.

The drawbacks of the dehydrator are that it can take a long time and you have to be really careful with delicate ingredients to make sure they don't become stuck to the ring inside. When dehydrating, the hot air rises from the bottom, so it's also a good idea to rotate the rings now and again so that the material at the bottom doesn't dehydrate too fast.

Separatory Funnel

The separatory funnel is a fantastic bit of kit because it can separate two liquids with different densities – an extremely useful tool when making hydrosols. In contrast to alcohol-based oils, which can interfere with the structure of the drink, water-based hydrosols are perfect for introducing subtle flavours in cocktails. The first hydrosol I ever made was jasmine and I used it in a delicious rice-based cocktail in 2009. I was astonished by how quickly I could achieve fantastic results. It's incredibly simple: just pour your chosen two liquids into the funnel, and as the lighter liquid floats to the top it flavours the more dense liquid as it passes. For example, to make a mint hydrosol:

1. Combine mint oil with mineral water.

2. Shake vigorously.

3. Pour into the funnel.

4. Wait while the oil gradually floats to the top; as it does it will flavour the water.

5. Turn the valve and siphon off the water below, leaving the oil at the top.

Depending on the oils and how much flavour you want, you can use this method to make a really punchy hydrosol by leaving the two liquids for longer, or a lighter hydrosol over a shorter amount of time.

Heat Stirrer

The heat stirrer is really useful for mixing together ingredients with a constant, permeating temperature. It has a heated glass panel on the top and a magnetic beam that spins around so that it can heat consistently without need for manual stirring. When I first started working with fine gelatine in 2006, I found the heat stirrer to be invaluable. Gelatine is comprised of a series of protein chains; to open them up they need a constant heat source as well as agitation. If you simply tried to heat gelatine over an induction heater, the material at the bottom would open up in one lump, but when stirred constantly, all the protein chains open up simultaneously and this ensures that the gel has no lumps.

Micron Pipette

Essential oils are an integral ingredient in many of my cocktail recipes. I first started to explore their potential when researching how perfumers put together their scents and realised just how intensely accurate you had to be. These oils are comprised of highly concentrated flavours and, consequently, using micron pipettes – which measure to 1/1000th of a millilitre – is the only way to accurately control your effect on the overall flavour of a product. It lends an unparalleled level of precision to using essential oils – squidgy pipettes just don't hack it!

The micron pipettes are used every day in my lab to compound fragrances and to make bar prep more efficient by adding essences directly into their respective bottles: Dry Essence Tincture (page 186) to dry vermouth, cassis into Silver Needle tea, lime and salivating mix (page 220) to cachaça. They also lend the lab an air of CSI...

Homogeniser

A homogeniser is a machine that transforms the consistency of a substance by breaking up its particles, resulting in a more uniform, or homogenous, product. There are several types of homogeniser used in the food industry and in science laboratories, but the one we use in the Drink Factory lab is a simple model that works using a series of fast-spinning sharp blades. I use this piece of kit for every fresh juice that I make, especially for more fibrous juices such as lemon, lime and rhubarb. When the blades spin, they break up the fibres of the juice, which produces a rounder, fuller, richer flavour. There are different levels on the homogeniser so that you can choose the speed at which the blades spin. The more fibrous the juice, the higher the level needed. However, be careful not to homogenise a juice for too long at too high a speed, or it will begin to burn. The homogeniser is incredibly useful when making batches of juice because it reduces the variance between each batch.

Refractometer

The refractometer is a hand-held device that I use to measure the concentration of alcohol levels. It works along the principle of refraction – measuring the degree to which light changes direction when passing through a liquid.

It is incredibly useful to know the exact alcohol percentage of my cocktails so that I can truly understand how they work. I started making homemade liqueurs in 2008 and to ensure consistency of product I bought a basic refractometer with a glass slider. Later I moved on to an electronic one, which is more accurate and easier to read with darker liquids. Later, when I first started distilling using the Rotavapor, I had to make sure that the ABV of the distillate was at 40 per cent rather than the 70 per cent at which it first comes off. To lower it, I add water until it reaches the desired level on the refractometer. It's an essential piece of equipment for ensuring accuracy.

Thermomix

The Thermomix is the ultimate blender – with titanium blades it is incredibly powerful and can blend any number of hard ingredients into a superfine powder. Powders are useful because they have more surface area, which means more flavour can be extracted from the product. I've used the Thermomix for making powders from bits of barrel stave or nutmegs and without a doubt the fresher the powder the more flavourful the product.

The Thermomix is also incredibly efficient because it has a heating element. This allows you to make purées by combining your ingredients directly in the Thermomix, then simply setting the heat and letting it spin. The resulting blend is fantastic because it cooks consistently as it rotates. Temperature control means that you can keep a drink in it at a very specific temperature and serve it straight out of the Thermomix – so practical and accurate!

Brix Meter

The Brix meter is a small, usually hand-held device for measuring the amount of sugar in liquids or fruits – the bigger the sugar crystals, the higher the reading. Brix meters are extensively used in the wine-making industry and by farmers for testing the sugar content of grapes, fruit and vegetables to help determine the best time for their harvest. This ensures that the products reach consumers in their most perfect state or that they are ready for the process of vinification.

There are a couple of different types of Brix meter; I first purchased a basic model in 2008 that had a glass slider, but soon moved on to an electronic one with a laser that refracts off the glass plate. In addition to being more accurate, it also allows me to measure brown spirits, which had previously been hard to get a reading from as their colour obscured the plate.

I use the Brix every day to test stock syrups, cordials, purées and liqueurs so that I achieve the same results every time. I also use the Brix each time we cook fruit and spirits sous vide. The sugar content in fruit is a major factor in the final flavour and consequently I test each box – fruits harvested at different times of the year, or from different regions, vary wildly, affecting the outcome of the infusion and any cocktail that they may later be used in. We use sugar as an ingredient in cocktails so often, without really knowing much about its effect. The more information we have about cocktails, the better we can understand how they work. The Brix meter is a truly worthwhile investment if you are making your own ingredients, probably the most important bit of kit in which I've ever invested!

Rotavapor

The Rotavapor is an instrument used to distil a solvent. The purpose of distillation is to separate a given mixture into its components based on their respective volatilities, through the process of evaporation and condensation. What makes the Rotavapor so fantastic is that it has a vacuum. This allows you to evaporate things at lower boiling points because you're evaporating through pressure rather than heat. This is incredibly useful because the less heat you use, the less likely you are to damage or pull apart the more delicate volatiles of an ingredient. Alcohol is a fantastic medium for carrying flavour and volatile aromas. You can extract the purest and freshest flavours from ingredients by removing the water and replacing with a solvent such as alcohol, gently and at low temperatures. This means your final product has a fuller spectrum of aroma and flavour notes.

The rotation of the evaporating flask, immersed in a heated water bath, increases the surface area of the product, greatly speeding up distillation and also, through forced convection, keeping the mixture evenly mixed and heated, to promote stable, even evaporation. For example, when distilling rose petals, you have very delicate, small molecules, which too much heat would simply burn. With less heat, the delicate molecules are preserved and come through along with the bigger molecules. In this way you have the big picture of what a rose is. What I love about the Rotavapor is that it is one of the most complicated pieces of equipment used in the lab but the products made from it are incredibly poetic.

Chiller

The chiller is an attachment that I employ every time the Rotavapor is used. This piece of kit reduces the temperature of the coils in the Rotavapor distillation, which means that it condenses the evaporating liquid more efficiently – the lower the temperature, the better the condensation, otherwise the mixture begins to evaporate out. It's like a cat-and-mouse game with volatiles – the trick is to not let the small molecules get away so that as much as possible of the whole flavour comes through. The difference between the distillations with and without is remarkable!

Peristaltic Pump

A good friend of mine, Dave Arnold is the head of the food technology department at the French Culinary Institute, New York. The peristaltic pump is an attachment to the Rotavapor that he rigged up for us at the Drink Factory. One of the problems that occurs the first time you distil an ingredient that you've not tried before is that you don't know where to cut (stop) the distillation. The peristaltic pump allows me to cut the heads and tails from the Rotavapor vacuum still without breaking the seal and thereby losing an enormous amount of volatiles. This allows you to pull off parts of the ingredient to see where the best concentration of flavours are, without compromising the final flavour of the distillation.

7.

JUICES

Introduction ───────────────────────────── ●

Fresh juices are imperative to the cocktail formula. Freshly pressed always tastes better: by keeping it à la minute or as close to service as possible, the flavour is more natural and more intense. All fresh juices quickly lose their potency and impact, even if they are bottled and sealed in the fridge, so whether I'm using the juice for service in the bar or at home I never keep the bottle for more than 24 hours. Once pressed I use a homogeniser to give a cleaner edge to the flavour but this is an optional extra for the following recipes.

Orange & Clementine Juice

Yield: 500ml

1. Remove five pieces of zest from the oranges.

2. Juice the oranges and clementines respectively – aim for 100ml of clementine juice and 400ml of orange juice. .

3. Express the oils from the orange zest by twisting the slices over the juice.

4. Homogenise the juice in four 20-second blasts.

INGREDIENTS
— 6 organic oranges
— 10 organic clementines

EQUIPMENT
— Knife
— Chopping board,
— Juicer
— Homogeniser
— Micron pipette

Pink Grapefruit Juice

Yield: 400ml

1. Remove five slices of zest from the grapefruits, avoiding the pith

2. Slice the grapefruits in half and juice them

3. Express the oils from the zest by twisting the slices over the juice.

4. Homogenise the juice in four bursts of 25 seconds.

5. Add the nootkatone using a micron pipette and stir to mix.

INGREDIENTS
— 8 large organic pink grapefruits
— 5 microns of nootkatone

EQUIPMENT
— Knife
— Chopping board,
— Juicer
— Homogeniser

Tarragon Juice

Yield: 1g

1. Put the tarragon through a microjuicer.

2. Strain using a Superbag (page 221).

INGREDIENTS
— 30g fresh tarragon

EQUIPMENT
— Microjuicer
— 100-micron Superbag

Grilled Lemon Juice

Yield: 100ml

1. Chop the lemons in half and grill under a medium heat until golden brown.

2. Juice the grilled lemons.

3. Strain using a Superbag (page 221).

4. Homogenise in four 25-second bursts.

INGREDIENTS
— 5 Sicilian lemons

EQUIPMENT
— Knife
— Chopping board
— Grill
— Juicer
— 100-micron Superbag
— Homogeniser

Clear Lemon

Yield: 300ml

1. Heat 125ml of the lemon juice with the agar-agar in a pan on the induction heater at 95°C.

2. Stir until the agar dissolves.

3. Take off the heat, add the remaining 250ml of lemon juice and whisk together.

4. Seal the juice in a vacuum bag and place in the freezer overnight.

5. Once frozen, remove from the freezer and place the block of frozen juice in a funnel lined with a coffee filter and allow to defrost in a jug. The clear juice will drip through as the block melts.

6. Strain with a Superbag (see page 221).

INGREDIENTS
— 375ml fresh lemon juice
— 0.7g agar-agar

EQUIPMENT
— Measuring jug
— Small scales
— Pan
— Induction heater
— Whisk
— Vacuum machine and bag, funnel
— Coffee filter
— Jug
— 100-micron Superbag

Clear Lime

Yield: 300ml

1. Heat 125ml of the lime juice with the agar-agar in a pan on the induction heater at 95°C.

2. Stir until the agar dissolves.

3. Take off the heat and add the remaining 250ml of lime juice and whisk together.

4. Seal the juice in a vacuum bag and place in the freezer overnight.

5. Once frozen, remove from the freezer and place the block of frozen juice in a funnel lined with a coffee filter and allow to defrost in a jug. The clear juice will drip through as the block melts.

6. Strain with a Superbag (see page 221).

INGREDIENTS
— 375ml fresh lime juice
— 0.7g agar-agar

EQUIPMENT
— Measuring jug
— Small scales
— Pan
— Induction heater
— Whisk
— Vacuum machine
  and bag
— Jug
— Funnel
— Coffee filter
— 100-micron Superbag

Tomato Mix

Yield: 2 litres

1. Make a paste of the barley miso by adding the tablespoon of water.

2. Mix with the tomato juice and passata until the miso paste has completely dissolved.

INGREDIENTS
— 20g barley miso
— 1 tbsp mineral water
— 1 litre organic
  tomato juice
— 1 litre passata

EQUIPMENT
— Large scales
— Tablespoon,
— Mixing bowl
— Measuring jug

8.

CORDIALS

Introduction ————————————————————— ●

Homemade cordials are an important method of control
for the bartender, who at all times must be considering
the balance of their drink. By making your own cordial
you can complement the flavour profile of all your drink's
ingredients; this way you are not just using what you
have to hand, but tailor-making a key ingredient. I have
often thought it to be a bad bartending mentality to use
only what is commercially available when it comes to
cordials – this is not a practice that you would see employed
by chefs, who always seem to be seeking veracity and control
of their ingredients. All cordials will keep for up to 3 weeks
in sealed glass bottles.

Lime Cordial

Yield: 1.9 litres

1. Combine the sugar and mineral water in a pan and bring to the boil on an induction heater.

2. Take off the heat and add the lime zest and juice.

3. Check that the Brix reading is 35 and slowly increase the sugar if not.

4. Add the citric acid and tartaric acid.

5. Chill in an ice-bath for 24 hours, then strain using a Superbag.

6. Bottle and store in the fridge.

INGREDIENTS
— 450g sugar
— 1.14 litres mineral water
— 10g lime zest
— 480ml fresh lime juice
— 14.25g citric acid
— 5.4g tartaric acid

EQUIPMENT
— Large and small scales
— Measuring jug
— Pan
— Induction heater
— Brix meter
— 100-micron Superbag
— Glass bottle

Gooseberry Cordial

Yield: 1.1 litres

1. Combine the gooseberry juice, mineral water and sugar in a pan.

2. Heat over an induction heater and bring the sweetness to 35 on a Brix meter.

3. Take off the heat and add the malic and tartaric acids.

4. Bottle and store in the fridge.

INGREDIENTS
— 375g gooseberry juice
— 375g mineral water
— 250g caster sugar
— 5g malic acid
— 2.2g tartaric acid

EQUIPMENT
— Large scales
— Jug
— Pan
— Induction heater
— Brix meter
— Small Scales
— Glass bottle

Rhubarb Cordial

Yield: 1.4 litres

1. Dice the rhubarb into bite-sized pieces and separate into three batches.

2. Place in vacuum bags and cook for 1 hour at 60°C in a bain-marie. Squeeze the bags in the middle of the process to break the veins of the rhubarb and release the flavours.

3. Blend the cooked rhubarb with the water in the Thermomix, then place in a centrifuge and spin at 5000 rpm for 10 minutes. Strain using a Superbag until only approximately 480ml of juice is left.

4. Heat the juice along with the sugar in a pan over an induction heater. Bring the sweetness to 35 on a Brix meter.

5. Add the malic acid.

6. Bottle and store in the fridge.

INGREDIENTS
— 1.1kg trimmed
  fresh rhubarb
— 1 litre mineral water
— 450g caster sugar
— 10g malic acid

EQUIPMENT
— Knife
— Chopping board
— Large scales
— Measuring jug
— Vacuum machine
  and bags
— Bain-marie
— Thermomix
— Centrifuge
— 100-micron
  Superbag
— Pan
— Induction heater
— Brix meter
— Glass bottle

Elderflower Cordial

Yield: 1.15 litres

1. Combine the sugar and mineral water in a pan and bring to the boil on the induction heater.

2. Take off the heat and add the lime zest and elderflowers.

3. Check that the Brix reading is 35 and increase the sugar if not.

4. Add the citric acid and tartaric acid.

5. Chill in an ice-bath for 24 hours, then strain using a Superbag.

6. Bottle and store in the fridge.

INGREDIENTS
— 450g sugar
— 1.14 litres mineral water
— 10g lime zest
— 100g fresh elderflowers
— 14.25g citric acid
— 5.4g tartaric acid

EQUIPMENT
— Large and Small Scales
— Measuring Jug
— Pan
— Induction heater
— Brix meter
— 100-micron Superbag
— Glass bottle

Nettle Cordial

Yield: 1.14 litres

1. Combine the sugar and mineral water in a pan and bring to the boil on an induction heater.

2. Add the nettle leaves to the water and stew for 10 minutes or until the water becomes golden. Be very careful not to burn or overcook the nettles. The result should be a light straw colour.

3. Check that the Brix level is 35 and increase the sugar if not.

4. Add the citric acid and tartaric acid.

5. Strain through a Superbag and bottle. Store in the fridge.

INGREDIENTS
— 450g caster sugar
— 1.14 litres mineral water
— 8g dried nettles
— 14.25g citric acid
— 5.4g tartaric acid

EQUIPMENT
— Large and small scales
— Measuring Jug
— Pan
— Induction heater
— Brix meter
— 100-micron Superbag
— Glass bottle

9.
WATERS
& MILKS

Introduction ———————————————————————————— ●

Flavoured waters and milks are a fantastic way of
introducing very soft, long and delicate flavours into drinks.
Simple, minimal and effective. The milks are at their best
for 24 hours, waters will keep for up to 3 days in sealed
glass bottles.

Almond Milk

Yield: 220ml

1. In a jug, mix the *pasta di mandorle* with the mineral water.

2. Pour the liquid into a Thermomix and blitz.

3. Strain using a Superbag.

Note:

If you're making this for use in the Almond Ramos recipe (page 40), you will need to measure it in grams, as specified. However, the yield produced here will be enough.

INGREDIENTS
— 62g *pasta di mandorle* (almond paste)
— 240g mineral water

EQUIPMENT
— Small scales
— Jug
— Thermomix
— 100-micron Superbag

Almond Milk Rice Water

Yield: 800ml

1. In a Thermomix, combine the mineral water with the rice and almond paste.

2. Blitz until liquid.

3. Strain using a Superbag.

4. Add the cedarwood essence with a micron pipette.

INGREDIENTS
— 700ml mineral water
— 200g sticky Japanese rice
— 30g *pasta di mandorle* (almond paste)
— 50 microns of cedarwood essence

EQUIPMENT
— Thermomix
— Measuring Jug
— Large scales
— 100-micron Superbag
— Micron Pipette

Tuberose Honey Water

Yield: 400ml

1. Weigh the honey and mix in a jug with the warm mineral water until fully dissolved.

2. Add the tuberose hydrosol with a micron pipette.

INGREDIENTS
— 200g Tasmanian honey
— 200g warm
    mineral water
— 2g tuberose hydrosol
    (for more information
    see page 107)

EQUIPMENT
— Large scales
— Jug
— Micron pipette

Silver Needle Tea

Yield: 700ml

1. Heat the mineral water in a pan over an induction heater until it reaches 80°C exactly.

2. Add the tea and let it brew for 7 minutes.

3. Take off the heat and add the cassis bud tincture.

4. Allow to cool before bottling.

INGREDIENTS
— 700ml mineral water
— 6g white Silver
    Needle tea
— 700 microns of cassis
    bud tincture

EQUIPMENT
— Measuring Jug
— Pan
— Induction Heater
— Thermometer
— Micron Pipette
— Glass bottle

Olive Water

Yield: 700ml

1. Put the whole olives into the centrifuge containers. Seal and spin at 4500 rpm for 10 minutes. Do this three times.

2. After each cycle (spin), drain the olive water and reseal the centrifuge containers.

INGREDIENTS
— 3.5kg green olives

EQUIPMENT
— Large scales
— Centrifuge

Olive Water

10.
DISTILLATIONS

Introduction ———————————————————— ●

Distillations are the ultimate bespoke ingredient to use
in a cocktail. They can make the most of entirely natural
ingredients, accommodating a wide band of flavours that
respect the original ingredient and avoid any artificial
flavourings. Flavours can be made to spec and with a specific
drink or concept in mind rather than building a concept
around an available product. Once you have the formula, it's
very easy to execute and replicate and the results are head
and shoulders above what you can buy commercially. I've
made my own distillations that not only work in my bar but
also as a stand-alone product.

Horseradish Vodka

Yield: 1 litre

1. Combine the horseradish and celeriac in a Thermomix and blend until the mixture is fine.

2. Mix with 700ml of the vodka and pour through a funnel into the Rotavapor flask.

3. Set up the Rotavapor and gradually lower the m-bars until it reaches 35.

4. Leave to distil until 500ml of liquid has been achieved.

5. Using the refractometer, rectify the ABV content to 40 with mineral water.

6. Combine 500ml of the horseradish vodka with the remaining 500ml of vodka.

INGREDIENTS
— 50g fresh horseradish
— 25g celeriac
— 1.2 litres vodka
— Mineral water, to adjust

EQUIPMENT
— Large scales
— Thermomix
— Measuring jug
— Funnel
— Rotavapor
— Refractometer

Parsley Vodka

Yield: 500ml+

1. Pick the parsley leaves from the stalks and add the leaves to the Rotavapor flask.

2. Pour the vodka through a funnel into the Rotavapor flask.

3. Set up the Rotavapor and gradually lower the m-bars until it reaches 35.

4. Leave to distil until 500ml of liquid has been achieved.

5. Using the refractometer, rectify the ABV content to 40 with mineral water.

INGREDIENTS
— 100g fresh
  flat-leaf parsley
— 700ml vodka
— Mineral water, to adjust

EQUIPMENT
— Large scales
— Rotavapor
— Measuring jug
— Funnel
— Refractometer

Pink Peppercorn Vodka

Yield: 300ml

1. Bruise the peppercorns with a pestle and mortar and put into the Rotavapor flask.

2. Pour the vodka through a funnel into the flask.

3. Set up the Rotavapor and gradually lower the m-bars until it reaches 35.

4. Leave to distil until 300ml of liquid has been achieved.

5. Using the refractometer, rectify the ABV content to 40 with mineral water.

INGREDIENTS
— 100g whole organic pink peppercorns
— 400ml vodka
— Mineral water, to adjust

EQUIPMENT
— Large scales
— Pestle and mortar
— Measuring jug
— Funnel
— Rotavapor
— Refractometer

Port Reduction

Yield: 250ml

1. Pour the port through a funnel into the Rotavapor flask.

2. Set up the Rotavapor and gradually lower the m-bars until it reaches 35.

3. Leave to distil until 500ml of liquid has been achieved.

4. Discard the 500ml of clear liquid and bottle the remaining port reduction.

INGREDIENTS
— 700ml ruby port

EQUIPMENT
— Measuring jug
— Funnel
— Rotavapor
— Glass bottle

Pink Peppercorns in Rotavapor Flask

11.
LIQUEURS & SYRUPS

Introduction ————————————————————●

I first started making my own syrups in 1999 so that I could have a whole array of flavours at my fingertips that weren't commercially available at the time. Once I started experimenting with recipes, I found that I could produce more intense and fresher flavours. Depending on the particular cocktail in which they were used, I could go on to modify the syrup according to the drink.

Later advances in technology made the syrups more accurate, more efficient and faster to make than ever before. It was then that I began to apply the same processes to making my own liqueurs. It's very important that you get the same Brix reading (sugar level) for each batch of syrup or bottle of liqueur (see page 160). Both the homemade syrups and liqueurs have a more natural and wider band of flavour, with no artificial flavourings or colourings. They're the perfect bespoke ingredient to pack an extra punch in any drink.

Orgeat (Almond Syrup)

Yield: 2.2 litres

1. Put the almonds in a Thermomix and blend until they become powder.

2. Combine the powder in a mixing bowl with the mineral water and orange blossom water and leave to sit for 2 hours, stirring occasionally.

3. Using a Superbag, strain the almond mix into a pan, in order to separate the pulp from the water. Discard the pulp.

4. Add the sugar to the pan of almond water and, on a low heat (level 3 for an induction heater), stir until the sugar has dissolved.

5. Homogenise for 30 seconds at full power.

6. Bottle and store in the fridge.

Storage

Once opened, use within a week. Unopened, this will keep for up to 3 weeks if sealed and kept in the fridge.

INGREDIENTS
— 1kg plain almonds
— 1.6 litres mineral water
— 10ml orange
   blossom water
— 1.4kg caster sugar

EQUIPMENT:
— Large scales
— Thermomix
— Mixing bowl
— Measuring spoons
— Jug
— 250-micron Superbag
— Pan
— Induction heater
— Homogeniser
— Glass bottles

Liquorice Syrup

Yield: 1 litre

1. In a pan, combine the liquorice powder and mineral water, mix well and then add the sugar.

2. Heat on an induction heater at level 4 for 10 minutes. Remove the scum as it forms.

3. Once all the sugar is dissolved, bottle and leave to cool.

Storage

Once opened, use within a week. Unopened, this will keep for up to 3 weeks if sealed and kept in the fridge.

INGREDIENTS
— 40g liquorice powder
— 500ml mineral water
— 750g caster sugar

EQUIPMENT:
— Pan
— Large scales
— Measuring Jug
— Induction heater
— Glass bottles

Raspberry & Violet Syrup

Yield: 700ml

1. In a mixing bowl, dissolve the violet essence in the pure alcohol.

2. Add the mix to the bottle of raspberry syrup. Seal and keep refrigerated. Use within 1 week.

INGREDIENTS
— 7 microns of violet essence
— 2g pure alcohol
— 1 x 700ml bottle of raspberry syrup

EQUIPMENT
— Mixing bowl
— Small scales
— Micron pipette

Mallow Syrup

Yield: 600ml

1. Scrape the seeds from the vanilla pod into a bowl and discard the pod.

2. Combine all the ingredients in a vacuum bag and seal in the vacuum machine.

3. Cook sous vide in a bain-marie for 30 minutes at 60°C.

4. Strain using a Superbag. Use within 1 week.

INGREDIENTS
— 1 vanilla pod
— 25g mallow root
— 400ml mineral water
— 400g sugar

EQUIPMENT
— Knife
— Large scales
— Measuring jug
— Vacuum machine and bag
— Bain-marie
— 100-micron Superbag

Homemade Amaretto

Yield: 700ml

1. Crush the amaretti biscuits and steep in vodka for 2 days.

2. Combine the biscuit mix in a pan with the sugar. Place on the induction heater over a very low heat until the sugar has dissolved.

3. Strain through a Superbag then bottle.

INGREDIENTS
— 200g amaretti biscuits
— 500ml vodka
— 120g sugar

EQUIPMENT
— Large scales
— Measuring jug
— Pan
— Induction heater
— 100-micron Superbag

Rose Vodka

Yield: 600ml

1. Combine all the ingredients in a mixing bowl.

2. Stir to dissolve then bottle.

INGREDIENTS
— 500ml vodka
— 5ml Arabica rose water
— 200g caster sugar
— 2ml tuberose hydrosol
  (for more information see
  page 107)

EQUIPMENT
— Measuring spoons
  and jug
— Large scales
— Mixing bowl

Homemade Grenadine

Yield: 1.5 litres

1. Combine the pomegranate juice and sugar in a pan.

2. Heat on the induction heater at level 4 for 10 minutes. Stir continuously.

3. Allow to cool then bottle.

Storage

Once opened, use within a week. Unopened, this will keep for up to 3 weeks if sealed and kept in the fridge.

INGREDIENTS
— 1 litre fresh organic pomegranate juice
— 1.45kg sugar

EQUIPMENT
— Measuring jug
— Large scales
— Pan
— Induction heater
— Glass bottle

Rhubarb Liqueur

Yield: 1.5 litres

1. In a pan on the induction heater, dissolve the sugar in the rhubarb juice over a low heat.

2. Add the vodka, malic and tartaric acids and stir.

3. Add the rose hydrosol then bottle.

INGREDIENTS
— 500g sugar
— 480g rhubarb juice
— 1kg vodka
— 10g malic acid
— 4.4g tartaric acid
— 1g tube rose hydrosol (for more information see page 107)

EQUIPMENT
— Pan
— Induction heater
— Large and small scales

Salted Caramel Liqueur

Yield: 300ml

1. In a pan on an induction heater, make the caramel by combining the sugar and mineral water. Heat on level 10 at 170°C for 12 minutes.

2. Take off the heat and add the salt and malic acid. Stir.

3. Add to a Thermomix, and set at 50°C.

4. Mix on power 2 for 15 minutes.

5. Add the vodka and allow the liqueur to cool completely.

Storage

Once opened, the liqueur will last for 4 weeks if kept refrigerated. Unopened, the liqueur will keep for up to 2 months in the fridge. If unsure, check the aroma – the liqueur will cease to smell once it is past its best.

INGREDIENTS
— 250g sugar
— 10ml mineral water
— 2.5g Mexican salt
— 1g malic acid
— 250g vodka

EQUIPMENT
— Pan
— Induction heater
— Small scales
— Measuring spoon
— Thermomix
— Temperature probe

12.
TINCTURES & ESSENCES

Introduction ————————————————————— ●

Tinctures and essences are small in volume but huge in flavour. They work on the principle of reduction; by simply combining any ingredient in a high volume of liquid and then reducing it down, it becomes highly concentrated and expands inside the liquid before it disperses. When you add that to a drink the flavours re-animate and enlarge, emitting a more dense, concentrated and powerful flavour. Essences are incredibly subtle and are a fantastic way to carry beautiful, esoteric flavours within a drink. Very high food-grade essential oils provide the base of these essences; the purer they are, the better, and the easier they are to blend. These essential oils allow me to access flavours that would be near impossible to make myself. The result is a clean mixture of ingredients that echoes the methods of perfumers for a truly unique ingredient.

It is really important if you are going to use food-grade essences that all the information about food safety and proportions is diligently read. If stored in cool, dry place in tightly sealed apothecary bottles, tinctures and essences will last for up to 1 year.

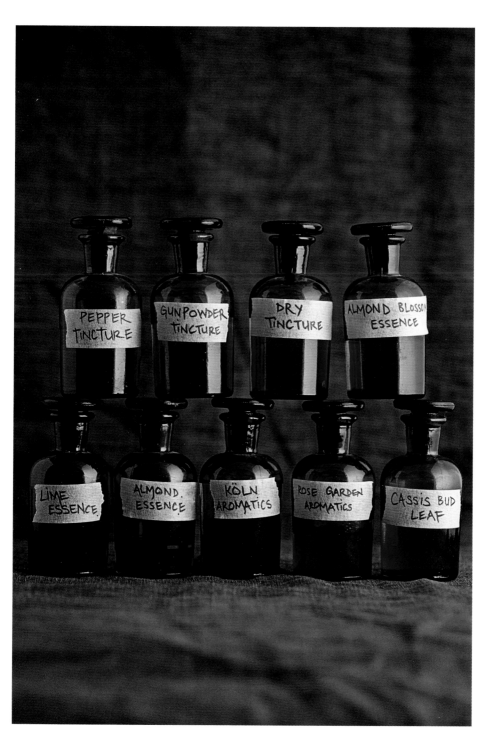

Tinctures

Dry Essence Tincture

Yield: 75g

1. Combine both ingredients in a mixing bowl, transfer into a sealed container and leave for 2 weeks.

2. Set up a Rotavapor, add the mixture and gradually lower the m-bars until it reaches 35.

3. Distil until you have reduced the liquid to 50 per cent.

4. Strain with a Superbag.

INGREDIENTS
— 150g pure alcohol
— 16 capsules of
   grape-seed extract

EQUIPMENT
— Large scales
— Mixing bowl
— Rotavapor
— 100-micron Superbag

Pepper Tincture

Yield: 100ml

1. Blend the black peppercorns in a Thermomix until they become a fine powder.

2. Combine the pepper and pure alcohol in a glass jar.

3. Seal the jar and leave to rest for 2 weeks.

4. Set up a Rotavapor, add the mixture and gradually lower the m-bars until it reaches 35.

5. Distil until the liquid has reduced by half.

6. Strain with a Superbag.

INGREDIENTS
— 500g black peppercorns
— 1 litre pure alcohol

EQUIPMENT
— Large scales
— Thermomix
— Measuring jug
— Glass jar
— Rotavapor
— 100-micron Superbag

Rose Garden Aromatics

Yield: 10g+

1. Place the 10g of pure alcohol into an antique aromatics jar.

2. Add the oils and essences one by one using the pipette.

3. Seal the jar and gently shake to mix.

4. Leave for 6 weeks.

Comments and notes:

It is very important that the jar is sterilised and that the measurements are exact. Change the nozzle for each different oil.

INGREDIENTS
— 10g pure alcohol
— 25 microns of Bulgarian rose otto
— 6 microns of Egyptian jasmine
— 8 microns of ambrette seed
— 7 microns of blackcurrant bud
— 6 microns of sandalwood oil
— 3 microns of dry tincture (page 186)
— 2 microns of patchouli
— 2 microns of cedar
— 2 microns of cedarwood oil

EQUIPMENT
— Small scales
— Antique aromatics jar
— 1–20 micron pipette

Cassis Bud Leaf Tincture

Yield: 50ml

1. Combine both ingredients in a mixing bowl.

Comments and notes:

700 microns of the tincture is added to a 700ml bottle of Silver Needle tea for use in the Silver Mountain (page 136).

(page 136)

INGREDIENTS
— 0.1g cassis bud leaf
— 50ml pure alcohol

EQUIPMENT
— Small scales
— Measuring jug
— Mixing bowl
— 1–20 micron pipette

Gunpowder Tincture

Yield: 100g

1. Combine both ingredients in a vacuum bag, seal and cook sous vide in a bain-marie at 60°C for 30 minutes.

2. Remove and strain through a Superbag.

INGREDIENTS
— 8g gunpowder tea pellets
— 100g pure alcohol

EQUIPMENT
— Vacuum machine
   and bag
— Bain-marie
— 100-micron Superbag

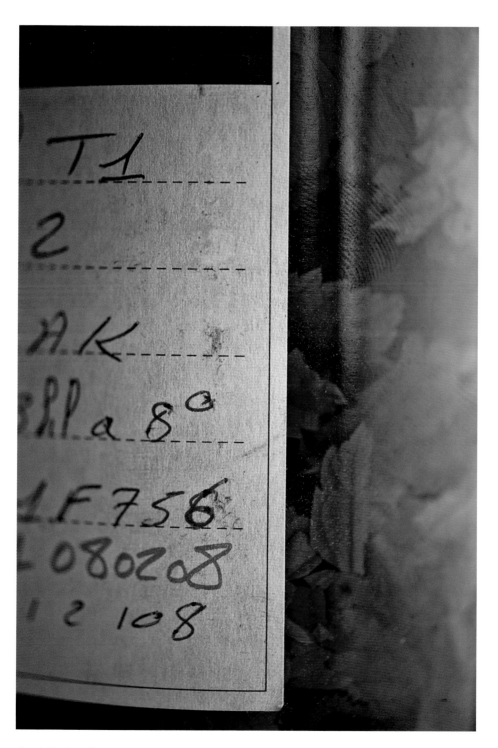

Cassis Bud Leaf Tincture

Koln Aromatics

Yield: 20g+

1. Put the 20g pure alcohol into a jar.

2. Add the oils and essences one by one using the pipette.

3. Seal the jar and gently shake to mix.

4. Leave for 3 weeks.

Comments and notes:

It is very important that the jar is sterilised and that the measurements are exact. Change the nozzle for every new oil or essence used. Based on a tincture in Jerry Thomas' *Bartender's Guide*, 2nd edition.

INGREDIENTS
— 20g pure alcohol
— 21 microns of bitter orange oil
— 2 microns of neroli oil
— 6 microns of petit grain oil
— 3 microns of rosemary essence
— 63 microns of rose water
— 2 microns of sandalwood oil
— 20 microns of lemon essence

EQUIPMENT
— Small scales
— Antique aromatics jar
— 1–20 micron pipette

Lime Essence

Yield: 25g

1. Place the pure alcohol into a jar and add the essence with a micron pipette.

2. Screw on the lid and shake to mix.

INGREDIENTS
— 25g pure alcohol
— 500 microns of food-grade lime oil

EQUIPMENT
— Small scales
— Glass jar
— 1–20 micron pipette

Almond Essence

Yield: 250g

1. Put the skinned almonds into a microjuicer with an oil-attachment, which will separate the pulp and oil.

2. Keep the oil and add the alcohol to it.

INGREDIENTS
— 250g skinned almonds
— 40g pure alcohol

EQUIPMENT
— Large and small scales
— Microjuicer

Almond Blossom Essence

Yield: 40g

1. Put the pure alcohol in a mixing bowl and add the essences and oils one by one using a micron pipette.

INGREDIENTS
— 40g pure alcohol
— 50 microns of bitter almond oil
— 2 microns of galbanum
— 2 microns of ambrettolide

EQUIPMENT
— Small scales
— Mixing bowl
— 1–20 micron pipette

Homemade Grapefruit Bitters

Yield: 600g

1. In a mixing bowl, combine all the ingredients except the pure alcohol.

2. Blitz in a Thermomix in 100g batches, for 1 minute at a time on full power.

3. Once all the batches have been blended, combine in a vacuum bag, add the pure alcohol and seal.

4. Cook sous vide in a bain-marie at 60°C for 30 minutes.

5. Use a Superbag to squeeze out all the excess liquid, then bottle.

INGREDIENTS
— 75g Sencha tea powder
— 7g ground sandalwood
— 100g raisins
— 60g pink grapefruit zest
— 38g pink grapefruit flesh
— 38g bitter orange essence
— 60g galanga root, grated
— 20g orris root, grated
— 5g quassia bark chips
— 2 vanilla pods
— 25g cinnamon
   sticks, grated
— 0.2g powdered tannins
— 3g ground cloves
— 25g lemon zest
— 19g ground ginger
— 10g ground cardamom
— 10g ground nutmeg
— 25g homemade burnt
   caramel (page 209)
— 100g mineral water
— 50g pure alcohol

EQUIPMENT
— Large and small scales
— Mixing bowl
— Thermomix
— Vacuum machine
   and bag
— Bain-marie
— 100-micron Superbag

13.
FOAMS

P. 195 / Camomile Foam

Introduction ⎯⎯⎯⎯⎯⎯⎯⎯⎯⎯⎯⎯⎯⎯●

It was the chef Bruno Loubet who first prompted me to spark a correspondence with Ferran Adrià, asking questions about his ideas and cocktail-making. This communication was to become, in essence, what stimulated me to scratch beneath the surface of what a cocktail was and could be. The subsequent correspondence built over the years has enabled me to understand his original techniques, but also to create new ones, some using the simple basics of science and others far more complex.

When I journeyed to Spain and the infamous El Bulli in 2004, Adrià was incredibly forthcoming, showing me his cocktail recipes: an open and transparent mentality that was really refreshing. It was interesting to apprehend drink-making at such an extremely high level through the lens of a chef rather than a bartender.

Foams were first conceived in 1998, when Adrià began working with cocktails and textures, and his creations struck me as both interesting and accessible. Foams are pure innovative pleasure. They combine both a new texture for the senses and a new way to deliver flavour – exaggerating but never exploiting it. It's hard not to love the theatrical element – when the drink is taken out, heads inevitability turn.

The basic recipe to create a foam uses gelatine and egg white as holding agents. The emulsion is transformed into a foam by charging it with gas in an ISI siphon. Carbon dioxide amplifies the notes put in the canister; small bubbles burst when drunk and release flavour. Once it leaves the siphon, the gelatine gels into a soft web that holds the bubbles from the gas.

I didn't want to replicate Adrià's methods exactly, but rather translate them from the kitchen to the bar. My criteria for creating a foam was high; it had to be delicate, beautiful to look at and smooth and silky when consumed. I wanted the foam to enhance the drink but keep its balance and contrast with the liquid below it. The two layers had to work in tandem.

An inevitable fact of creating foams for a cocktail is that the alcohol content affects the stability of the foam. I needed the foam to sit on the cocktail for the 10 minutes it usually takes for a cocktail to be consumed and I wanted to ensure that when the foam did finally disintegrate, it didn't leave a sticky mess on the glass. The protein, which works in gelatine to stabilise the bubbles in the foam, is attacked by the alcohol from underneath. To reconcile this I tested the pH level of the drink with a pH meter in order to regulate the cocktail's acidity. If the acid content is too high it breaks down the protein chains of the foam. I then used a refractometer to see how strong the alcohol was when in the actual cocktail.

With these findings I experimented with different gelatines, trying many variations in order to find the right consistency to keep the structure of the foam in place. Consequently, I removed the egg white entirely and replaced it with Ovoneve, a powdered egg white, which was not flavourful but worked better as a bonding agent. It also makes sure that the foam shrinks down the glass as it is drunk, leaving no mess behind.

Camomile Foam

Yield: 925g

1. Combine the mineral water with the gelatine, camomile, vanilla and gomme in a ceramic mixing bowl and gently stir.

2. Cover with cling film and heat on low for 2 minutes in a microwave.

3. Add the Ovoneve to the mix and use a hand blender to blend until a consistent texture is achieved.

4. Use a sieve and funnel to strain the mixture into a siphon.

5. Add the nitrous oxide, shake and then chill in the fridge for an hour.

INGREDIENTS
— 800ml mineral water
— 3 gelatine sheets
— 30g camomile powder
— 5ml vanilla extract
— 75ml gomme syrup
— 15g Ovoneve (powdered egg white)
— 1 N2O gas charger

EQUIPMENT
— Measuring jug
— Small scales
— Ceramic mixing bowl
— Clingfilm
— Microwave
— Hand blender
— Sieve
— Funnel
— Siphon

14.
MACERATIONS

Introduction _____ ●

A maceration is when the particles of an ingredient are
softened or broken up using alcohol in order to release
flavour and aroma. Although this works along the same
principles as cooking sous vide, macerations can sometimes
be preferable because it can be difficult to release the
essential oils of an ingredient at high temperatures.

White Truffle Vermouth

Yield: 700ml

1. Finely chop the white truffle.

2. Add to the dry vermouth and put in a sterilised, dry glass bottle.

3. Seal the bottle with tape and leave to steep for at least 2 weeks.

Comments and notes:

The longer the mix is left to steep, the more dramatic the result. You can use this bottle as a solera system for at least 2 months.

INGREDIENTS
— 1g white truffle
— 700ml dry vermouth

EQUIPMENT
— Small scales
— Knife
— Chopping board
— Measuring jug
— Glass bottle

Black Truffle Vermouth

Yield: 700ml

1. Finely chop the black truffle.

2. Add to the dry vermouth and put in a clean, dry glass bottle.

3. Seal the bottle with tape and leave to steep for at least 2 weeks, but ideally up to 3 months.

Comments and notes:

The longer the mix is left to steep, the more dramatic the result. You can use this bottle as a solera system for at least 2 months.

INGREDIENTS
— 2g black truffle
— 700ml dry vermouth

EQUIPMENT
— Small scales
— Knife
— Chopping board
— Measuring jug
— Glass bottle

15.
SOUS VIDE ALCOHOL

Grapefruit Gin

Yield: 500ml

1. Slice the grapefruit flesh and zest, ensuring all residual pith is removed.

2. Add all the ingredients to a vacuum bag and seal using the vacuum machine.

3. Put in a bain-marie at 60°C for 1 hour, then remove and chill.

4. Filter the mix using a Superbag.

5. Put in the centrifuge for 10 minutes at maximum speed (5000 rpm).

6. Filter again and bottle.

INGREDIENTS
— 200g grapefruit flesh
— 4 x 3cm pieces of
  grapefruit zest
— 500ml gin

EQUIPMENT
— Small scales
— Chopping board
— Knife
— Measuring jug
— Vacuum machine
  and bag
— Bain-marie
— 100-micron Superbag
— Centrifuge
— Glass bottle

Blood Orange Gin

Yield: 500ml

1. Slice the blood orange flesh and zest, ensuring all residual pith is removed.

2. Add all the ingredients to a vacuum bag and seal using the vacuum machine.

3. Put in a bain-marie at 60°C for 1 hour, then remove and chill.

4. Filter the mix using a Superbag.

5. Put in the centrifuge for 10 minutes at maximum speed (5000 rpm).

6. Filter again and bottle.

INGREDIENTS
— 200g blood orange flesh
— 4 x 3cm pieces of blood orange zest
— 500ml gin

EQUIPMENT
— Small scales
— Chopping board
— Knife
— Measuring jug
— Vacuum machine and bag
— Bain-marie
— 100-micron Superbag
— Centrifuge
— Glass bottle

Bitter Lemon Gin

Yield: 700ml

1. Slice the lemon flesh and zest, retaining the pith.

2. Add all the ingredients to a vacuum bag and seal using the vacuum machine.

3. Put in a bain-marie at 60°C for 1 hour, then remove and chill.

4. Filter the mix using a Superbag.

5. Put in the centrifuge for 10 minutes at maximum speed (5000 rpm).

6. Filter again and bottle.

INGREDIENTS
— 200g lemon flesh
— 5 x 3cm pieces of lemon zest
— 700ml gin

EQUIPMENT
— Small scales
— Chopping board
— Knife
— Measuring jug
— Vacuum machine and bag
— Bain-marie
— 100-micron Superbag
— Centrifuge
— Glass bottle

Raspberry Gin

Yield: 700ml

1. Put all the ingredients in a vacuum bag and seal using the vacuum machine.

2. Put in a bain-marie at 52°C for 1 hour, then remove and chill.

3. Filter the mix using a Superbag.

4. Put in the centrifuge for 10 minutes at maximum speed (5000 rpm).

5. Filter again and bottle.

INGREDIENTS
— 700ml gin
— 250g fresh raspberries
— 10ml sugar syrup

EQUIPMENT
— Measuring jug
— Small scales
— Vacuum machine
  and bag
— Bain-marie
— 100-micron Superbag
— Centrifuge
— Glass bottle

Basil Gin

Yield: 200ml

1. Add both ingredients to a vacuum bag and seal using the vacuum machine.

2. Put in a bain-marie at 52°C for 1 hour, then remove and chill.

3. Filter the mix using a Superbag and then bottle.

INGREDIENTS
— 200ml gin
— 2g fresh basil

EQUIPMENT
— Measuring jug
— Small scales
— Vacuum machine
  and bag
— Bain-marie
— 100-micron Superbag
— Glass bottle

Shiso Dry Vermouth

Yield: 200ml

1. Add both ingredients to a vacuum bag and seal using the vacuum machine.

2. Put in a bain-marie at 52°C for 1 hour, then remove and chill.

3. Filter the mix using a Superbag and then bottle.

INGREDIENTS
— 200ml Dry Vermouth
— 2g fresh shiso

EQUIPMENT
— Measuring jug
— Small scales
— Vacuum machine and bag
— Bain-marie
— 100-micron Superbag
— Glass bottle

Seaweed Vodka

Yield: 500g

1. Wash the seaweed.

2. Add both ingredients to a vacuum bag and seal using the vacuum machine.

3. Put in a bain-marie at 52°C for 20 minutes, then remove and chill.

4. Filter the mix using a Superbag and then bottle.

INGREDIENTS
— 100g seaweed
— 500g vodka

EQUIPMENT
— Large scales
— Jug
— Vacuum machine and bag
— Bain-marie
— 100-micron Superbag,
— Glass bottle

Wild Strawberry & Neroli Purée

Yield: 550g

1. Put the strawberries in a vacuum bag and seal using the vacuum machine.

2. Cook sous vide in the bain-marie at 60°C for 2 hours, then remove and chill.

3. Combine the strawberries with the rest of the ingredients in a mixing bowl.

4. Pass the final mix through a microjuicer to the make the purée.

5. Homogenise the purée until it has a fine consistency.

INGREDIENTS
— 500g strawberries
— 50ml fresh lemon juice
— 18 drops of Arabica orange blossom water
— 12 microns of neroli

EQUIPMENT
— Large and small scales
— Vacuum machine and bag
— Bain-marie
— Mixing bowl
— Measuring jug
— Micron pipette
— Transfer pipette
— Microjuicer
— Homogeniser

Pumpkin Purée

Yield: 700g

1. Peel the pumpkin with a sharp knife and chop into 2.5cm chunks.

2. Seal in a vacuum bag and cook sous vide in a bain-marie at 60°C for 2 hours, then remove and chill.

3. Pass the mix through a microjuicer to make the purée.

4. Homogenise the purée until it has a fine consistency.

5. Add the remaining ingredients and mix.

INGREDIENTS
— 500g pumpkin
— 200g sugar
— 0.5g ground nutmeg

EQUIPMENT
— Large and small scales
— Knife
— Chopping board
— Measuring jug
— Vacuum machine and bag
— Bain-marie
— Microjuicer
— Homogeniser

Cherry Blossom & Almond Purée

Yield: 580g

1. Put the cherries and cherry blossom liqueur in a vacuum bag and seal using the vacuum machine.

2. Cook sous vide in a bain-marie at 60°C for 2 hours, then remove and chill.

3. Pass the final mix through a microjuicer to the make the purée.

4. Homogenise the purée until it has a fine consistency, then stir in the almond essence.

INGREDIENTS
— 500g pitted
 fresh cherries
— 75g cherry
 blossom liqueur
— 5g almond essence

EQUIPMENT
— Large and small scales
— Vacuum machine
 and bag
— Bain-marie
— Micron pipette
— Mixing bowl
— Microjuicer
— Homogeniser

Pear & Green Tea Purée

Yield: 502g

1. Peel and core the pears.

2. Seal in a vacuum bag and cook sous vide in a bain-marie at 70°C for 2 hours, then remove and chill.

3. Add the matcha and pass the final mix through a microjuicer to the make the purée.

4. Homogenise the purée until it has a fine consistency.

INGREDIENTS
— 500g Williams pears
— 2g high-quality matcha

EQUIPMENT
— Large and small scales
— Vacuum machine
 and bag
— Bain-marie
— Mixing bowl
— Measuring jug
— Micron pipette
— Transfer pipette
— Microjuicer
— Homogeniser

Hot Pepper Sauce

Final Yield: 1.5 litres

Part 1: Chilli mix without wood

1. Chop the chillies and mix in a bowl with the salt
and vinegar.

2. Add to a vacuum bag, seal using a vacuum machine and
cook in a bain-marie at 40°C for 2 hours.

3. Remove the bag of chilli mix from the bain-marie and
place in a bowl of cold water until cool.

4. Empty the chilli mix from the bag and put through the
microjuicer. Repeat several times.

5. Strain through a Superbag.

INGREDIENTS
— 150g red chillies
— 150g green chillies
— 10g salt
— 100ml malt vinegar

EQUIPMENT:
— Small scales
— Knife
— Chopping board
— Mixing bowl
— Measuring jug
— Vacuum machine
  and bag
— Bain-marie
— Microjuicer
— 100-micron Superbag

Part 2: Chilli mix with wood

1. Chop the chillies and mix in a bowl with the salt, vinegar
and oak chips.

2. Add to a vacuum bag, seal with a vacuum machine and
cook in a bain-marie at 40°C for 6 hours.

3. Remove the bag from the bain-marie and place in a bowl
of cold water until cool.

4. Leave for 2 days.

5. Empty the chilli mix from the bag and put through the
microjuicer. Repeat several times.

6. Strain through a Superbag.

INGREDIENTS
— 1.2kg red chillies
— 1.2kg green chillies
— 75g salt
— 450ml malt vinegar
— 120g oak chips

EQUIPMENT
— Large and small scales
— Knife
— Chopping board
— Mixing bowl
— Measuring jug
— Vacuum machine
  and bag
— Bain-marie
— Microjuicer
— 100-micron Superbag

Part 3: The final mix

1. Measure the ingredients and combine in a mixing bowl.

2. Strain through the Superbag.

3. Repeat until all solid residues have disappeared.

4. Bottle.

INGREDIENTS
— 232ml Chilli mix
  without wood
— 1.64 litres Chilli mix
  with wood
— 75g salt
— 450ml malt vinegar
— 120g oak chips

EQUIPMENT
— Measuring jug
— Mixing bowl
— 100-micron Superbag
— Glass bottle

16.

MISCELLANEOUS

Introduction ●

Just as in the English language there are irregular verbs, the language of drinks produces its own oddities: ingredients that don't quite seem to fit in. This chapter houses ingredients and techniques that work in a very different way to the rest.

Homemade Lemon Sorbet

Yield: 500ml

1. Heat the mineral water in a pan on an induction heater and add the sugar.

2. Simmer and stir until the sugar has dissolved, then add the lemon juice and grated zest.

3. Continue to simmer and stir for several minutes and then take off the heat.

4. Once cool, strain through a Superbag into a shallow container.

5. Beat the egg whites with a whisk and fold into the mix.

6. Place in a freezer for up to 3–4 days before use.

INGREDIENTS
— 180ml mineral water
— 240ml sugar syrup
— 120ml fresh lemon juice
— Grated zest of 1 lemon
— 2 fresh egg whites

EQUIPMENT
— Measuring jug
— Pan
— Induction heater
— 100-micron Superbag
— Shallow container
— Mixing bowl
— Whisk

Burnt Caramel

Yield: 160g

1. Heat the sugar and water in a pan on an induction heater, on level 10 or at 170°C, for 12 minutes, stirring constantly.

2. Remove from the heat and stir in the malic acid.

3. Store in an air-tight, plastic container in a cool, dry place for up to 4 weeks.

INGREDIENTS
— 250g sugar
— 10ml mineral water
— 1g malic acid

EQUIPMENT
— Large and small scales
— Measuring jug
— Pan
— Induction heater

Gooseberry Gin

Yield: 700ml

1. Combine the gooseberries and gin in a vacuum bag and seal using the vacuum machine.

2. Cook in a bain-marie at 52°C for 40 minutes, then remove and chill.

3. Filter the mix using a Superbag.

4. Put in the centrifuge for 10 minutes at maximum speed (5000 rpm).

5. Filter again and bottle.

INGREDIENTS
— 150g fresh gooseberries
— 700ml gin

EQUIPMENT
— Small scales
— Measuring jug
— Vacuum machine
  and bag
— Bain-marie
— Superbag
— Centrifuge
— Glass bottle

Green Tea Incense

Yield: 25 individual incense cones

1. Mix the powders and juniper oil together in a bowl and slowly add water, stirring gently with a spatula, until a clay-like paste has been achieved.

2. Transfer the paste into the conical moulds and place in a dehydrator at 40°C for 24 hours.

3. Remove the incense cones from the mould and cook for a further 24 hours in the dehydrator.

4. Store in a sealed shallow container, away from any moisture for up to 1 year.

INGREDIENTS
— 100g makko powder
— 25g cedar wood powder
— 20g sandalwood powder
— 10g powdered green tea
— 2g cassia powder
— 100 microns juniper oil
— Approx. 25g
  mineral water

EQUIPMENT
— Mixing bowl
— Spatula
— Conical silicone moulds
— Dehydrator
— Shallow container
  with lid

Bobbing Apples

1. Using a melon baller, scoop 25 apple balls.

2. Place them in an open tray inside a vacuum machine, which will suck the juice and air out of them.

3. Mix the mineral water with the pectin, fructose, sorbic and malic acids and CIS-3-Hexenal.

4. Re-flood the vacuum chamber with the modified juice to create the bobbing apples.

Notes and comments:

If you have any of the liquid mix left over, it will last for 1 week.

— 2 Pink Lady apples
— 200ml mineral water
— 25g pectin
— 25g fructose
— 5ml sorbic acid
— 3g malic acid
— 100 microns of CIS-3-Hexenal (grass essence)

Equipment
— Melon baller
— Vacuum machine
— Measuring jug
— Measuring spoon
— Small scales

Homemade Lipstick

1. Grate the beeswax and carnauba wax.

2. Melt the waxes together in a double boiler (or in a heatproof bowl set over a pan of boiling water), and once fully melted add the jojoba oil and castor oil to them.

3. In a separate bowl, mix the colours together well, eliminating all lumps.

4. Add the colour to the wax mixture in the double boiler, and let the components infuse thoroughly.

5. Once the mixture begins to cool and thicken, pour it into a small, shallow container.

6. Put in the fridge to solidify.

7. When ready to use, roll the lipstick out onto a plastic sheet ready for using the lip-shaped rubber stamp (see the Lipstick Rose recipe, page 104).

INGREDIENTS

For the lipstick
— 25g beeswax
— 50g carnauba wax
— 2g jojoba oil
— 5g castor oil

For the colour
— 5g brilliant-red food-grade powder
— 8g deep-red food-grade powder
— 1g violet food-grade powder
— 1g titanium-white food-grade powder

EQUIPMENT
— Grater
— Heatproof bowl
— Mixing bowl
— Pan
— Small scales
— Induction heater
— Shallow container
— Acetate plastic sheet
— Rolling pin
— Lip-shaped rubber stamp

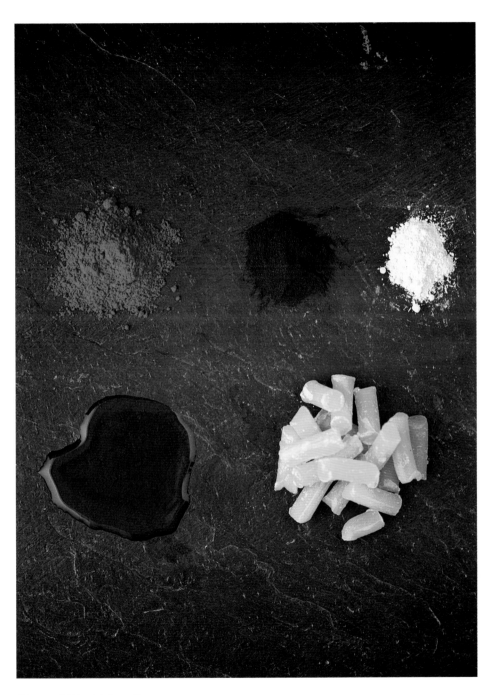

Homemade Lipstick Ingredients

17.
GLASSWARE

Introduction ⎯⎯⎯⎯⎯⎯⎯⎯⎯⎯⎯⎯⎯⎯ ●

Drinking is a sensual pleasure and the glass in which you
deliver a drink can make or break the enjoyment factor
of its contents. Aesthetics and the perception of taste are
interwoven; the visual aspect of the glass is very important
and a fine martini glass will produce an entirely different
aura when drinking a Martini than a mass-produced mould
will. Drinks do taste different in different glassware: the
weight, texture, thickness, raw material and shape are all
factors in the taste experience.

Years spent working in bars and serving the same style of
drink in different glassware have led to this collection of my
favourite styles and the majority of the recipes in this book
have been made with a particular glass in mind.

Small Coupette

Yield: 3.5oz

I have always felt that stirred-down drinks should be made with small proportions and consumed in three or four sips, ensuring that a drink stays perfectly cold right until the last drop. These 3.5oz coupettes are perfect; a large Martini that takes forever to drink will inevitability end up warm, and a warm Martini is pure blasphemy.

Large Coupette

Yield: 7.5oz

To serve shaken drinks, I favour these coupettes over a more traditional martini glass or goblet. They have a pleasant aesthetic curve that is particularly practical for drinking sours, the foam of which requires a large surface area so as not to dissipate quickly.

Highball

Yield: 11.25oz

My preferred highballs are reminiscent of glassware used in Italian cafés. More elegant than most styles available, the narrow glass allows the ice cubes to stack on top of one another.

Rocks Glass

For me, a good rocks glass is a simple style of tumbler that has clean, modern curves. Neither fancy nor ornate, the glass should never distract from the drink. I've found that 4.5oz are the perfect size to fill to the brim with ice so that it looks ready to pop out of the glass.

Champagne Flute

The champagne flute has been somewhat neglected of late in favour of serving champagne in coupettes. Champagne looks and feels more decadent supped from a coupette but there are scientific reasons why any drink with bubbles tastes better in a flute. A champagne flute has a smaller surface area and this concentrates the bubbles and the aroma upwards and towards your nose. The larger the surface area, the more the bubbles break and the more aroma lost as the alcohol volatiles escape and come into contact with the air.

Riedel Grappa Glass

This glass is great for controlling the way in which you inhale the aroma of a drink. Its slight convex lip allows aromatised champagnes to release their aromas just as they reach your nose. This glass is perfect for The Rose (see page 110), the aromatics of which would become trapped and therefore too intense if delivered in a traditional champagne flute.

Sake Glass

The sake glass is a small cylindrical vessel traditionally used in Japan for the serving of sake. They are designed to hold between 30–50ml and are perfect for sipping from.

Bibliography

Adrià, Ferran, Adrià, Albert & Solier, Julie. *El Bulli: 1998–2002*. Spain: ARA Libres, 2002.

Aftel, Mandy. *Essence & Alchemy: A Book Of Perfume*. London: Bloomsbury Publishing, 2001.

Baudelaire, Charles. *The Flowers of Evil*. New York: Oxford University Press, 1998.

Blumenthal, Heston. *The Big Fat Duck Cookbook*. London: Bloomsbury Publishing, 2008.

Burr, Chandler. *The Emperor of Scent*. UK: Arrow Books, 2004.

Embury, David. *The Fine Art of Mixing Drinks*. 1st ed. New York: Doubleday, 1948.

Degroff, Dale. *The Essential Cocktail: The Art of Mixing Perfect Drinks*. USA: Clarkson Potter, 2009.

De Mente, Lafayette Boye. *Kata: The Key to Understanding & Dealing with the Japanese*. Tokyo: Tuttle Publishing, 2003.

Dornenburg, Andrew & Page, Karen. *Culinary Artistry*. USA: John Wiley & Sons Inc, 1996.

Gagnaire, Pierre. *Reflections on Culinary Artistry*. New York: Stewart, Tabori & Chang, 2003.

Grieve, Mrs, M. *A Modern Herbal*. UK: Penguin, 1977.

Hemphill, Ian. *The Spice and Herb Bible: A Cook's Guide*. Australia: Pan Macmillan, 2000.

Johnson, Harry. *Bartender's Manual: Mixellany Commemorative Edition*. UK: Mixellany Limited, 2009.

Jones, Andrew. *The Aperitif Companion: A Connoisseur's Guide to the World of Aperitifs*. New York: Knickerbocker Press, 1998.

LaVey, Szandor Anton. *The Devil's Notebook*. San Francisco, C.A: Feral House, 1992.

Meier, Frank. *The Artistry of Mixing Drinks*. Paris: Fryam Press, 1936.

McGee, Harold. *On Food and Cooking*. New York: Scribner, 1984.

Plato. *The Republic*. UK: Penguin, 2003.

This, Hervé & Gagnaire, Pierre. *Cooking: The Quintessential Art*. London: University of California Press, 2008.

Thomas, Jerry. *The Bartender's Guide: How to Mix Drinks*. 2nd ed. New York: Dick & Fitzgerald, 1862.

Turin, Luca. *The Secret of Scent: Adventures in Perfume and the Science of Smell*. London: Faber and Faber, 2006.

Turin, Luca & Sanchez, Tania. *Perfumes: The A-Z Guide*. New York: Penguin, 2009.

Wondrich, David. *Imbibe! from Absinthe Cocktail to Whiskey Smash, A Salute in Stories*. New York: Perigee Books, 2007.

Wondrich, David. *Punch: The Delights and Dangers of the Flowing Bowl*. New York: Perigee Books, 2010.

Glossary

Affila sprig part of the cress family, an attractive- looking vegetable that has a mild nutty taste.

Agar-agar a gelling agent derived from seaweed that retains its gelling properties up to a temperature of 80°C.

Angelica an earthy, bittersweet herb with a flavour reminiscent of juniper.

Bruising similar to muddling but more gentle.

Building to construct a drink over ice directly inside the glass in which it is served rather than in a shaker or cocktail tin.

Cassis bud the bud of the blackcurrant plant. It has an earthy, sulphuric and mineral taste.

Cassia bark a tropical evergreen tree, the bark of which (when ground) has a flavour akin to cinnamon but with a more bitter aftertaste.

Clarify the act of making a liquid clear.

Dewar flask a thermal container in which to keep liquid nitrogen safely.

Dry-shaking shaking sours drinks without ice. This is a binding method that allows the protein chains of the egg white to stretch more giving you a better foam on top of the final drink.

Florence fennel part of the fennel family, this aromatic herb has a mild anise-like flavour with a sweet aftertaste.

Heads and tails the result of any distillation is divided into three separate parts in the following order: heads, hearts and tails. The best and desired portion of the distillation is obtained from the hearts. Cut-off points have to be determined between heads, hearts and tails - the art lies in judging when to start collecting the hearts and when to stop.

Homogenise the act of breaking up the fibres of an ingredient. See page 158.

Hydrosol a water-based essence that suspends essential oils inside water through the process of distillation.

Hyssop a small, bushy aromatic plant of the mint family with distinct, bitter leaves.

Juniper a spicy, flowery herb with a pine-like, resinous taste.

Magician's wool a ball of cotton wool soaked in a dry, flammable nitrocellulose liquid. When lit, the cotton ball completely disappears with a magical puff.

Makko a Japanese binding agent made from the bark of evergreen trees, native to South East Asia.

Melissa an aromatic herb also known as lemon balm.

Micron pipette a pipette that measures in microns (1000th of a gram). They are invaluable for measuring incredibly small amounts of liquid accurately (see also page 158).

Nookatone a natural organic compound and aromatic of grapefruit.

Orris root a spice derived from irises grown in the eastern Mediterranean region, with a distinct floral, yet bitter, taste with an aroma of violets.

Quassia bark the bark of a bitter herb indigenous to South America.

Rinsing a glass the action of pouring a liquid over ice in a glass, swirling the liquid with a bar spoon and then discarding both liquid and ice. This leaves a subtle hint of flavour and aroma on the glass.

Ruscus an evergreen shrub with attractive but flavourless inedible leaves.

Sous-vide cooking ingredients with the use of a vacuum-machine and bain-marie. See page 148.

Siphon a utensil originally designed to whip cream and used in modern professional kitchens for the making of foams.

Salivating mix a liquid that increases the amount of saliva produced in the mouth.

Shochu a clear, distilled Japanese spirit, usually made from sweet potato or rice.

Stringer a zester that produces strings and is often used for garnishes.

Sugar syrup all recipes using sugar syrup have been made with 2 parts cane syrup to 1 part water.

Sugaring/salting the rim of a glass the action of moistening the rim of the glass with a slice of citrus fruit and running the rim over a plate of sugar or salt.

Superbag a very fine mesh bag through which liquids can be strained and clarified.

Transfer pipette a piece of equipment used to transport a measured volume of liquid.

Tuberose a root from the same family as the agave plant with essential oils that are traditionally used in perfume.

Twist a small piece of peel with the pith removed, twisted over a drink in order to release the oil. It is then usually dropped in a drink as a garnish. If the recipe calls for the twist to be discarded twist the zest over the drink but do not use as a garnish.

Vetiver grass a grass mostly found in Africa, it has a fresh, woody scent. wIts oil has real staying power on the skin and is often used in perfumes.

Volatiles molecules that easily evaporate at normal temperatures and pressures.

Xanthan gum a product derived from fermented starch, used as a thickening agent and to maintain solids in suspension within a liquid.

Index

Acknowledgements

Adam 'there's a rumour' Peters-Ennis, Addie 'Chin' Chinn & Sarianne
Plaisant, Alessandro 'la minchia' Boneschi, Andreas 'the dude' Tsanos, Arthur
'gin shots!' Combe, Bayode & Claire 'it's a wicked suit' Oduwole, Ben 'speedo'
Reed, Ben 'beautiful' Williams, Cami 'it was your shoe love' Hobby-Limon,
Cara 'you dumb ass' Soronen, Cas 'it's a Korean' Oh, Chad 'lonestar' Solomon,
Charles 'pint of sake' Vexenat, Claudio ' el niño' Antonio, Dale 'back in the
1860's Degroff & Jill 'sit still!' Degroff, Dave 'otarded' Arnold, Dave 'the bar
dent' Wondrich, Desmond 'I've seen something like this before' Payne, Don
'these are some of my favourite things' Lee, Eric 'don't leave the room' Fossard,
Flavio 'bin 364!' Clementi, Fab 'who were those guys?' Limon, Frances 'I'm
his Mum' McKevitt, Gary 'breathe in, breathe out' Regan, Guillaume 'living
the dream' Le Dorner, Giacamo 'si professor' Russo, Giles ' well, you know'
Gavin-Cowen, Hobby 'hellllooo' Limon, Ian 'more chilli' Morgan, Ingrid 'it's
done' Gordon, Jack 'I've got ice on my head' Robertiello, Jake 'this is how you
throw a dart' Burger, Jared & Anastasia 'you're naughty' Brown & Miller, Jeff
'did she just do that' Morgenthaler, Jenifer 'no ice! no fooking fruit!' Griffin,
John 'barf' Gakuru, Jim 'you're all slaves' Wood, Junior 'jun the trooper'
Romeo, James 'Jocky' Petrie, Kay 'Peter!' Dorelli, Kim 'Gargamel doesn't
exist' Ireland, Kenta 'hangover press-ups' Goto, Louisa 'am I drunk?' Gavin-
Cowen, Luc 'the cardboard box' Merlet, Maria 'Tonyeee you're late!' Ballester,
Marcis 'Byron' Dzelzainis, Meimi 'what bicycle' Sanchez, Melissa 'chewbacca'
Goodman, Marco 'I invented you something' Arrigo, Micky & Sammy 'what
shall we wear today?' McIlroy-Ross, Magga 'is it a man?' Kristjansdottir,
Mal 'you know who that is' Evans, Nick 'it has to be the 45' Strangeway,
Oliver 'do what you want' Peyton, Paul 'dirty' Weldon, Harold 'deliciousness'
McGee, Peter 'Rolling Stones' Dorrelli, Richie & Amanda 'I gotta tell you
something' Boccato, Sean 'darkside' Harrison, Shawn 'kismey' Kelley, Simon
'red wine' Knight, Simon 'the stunt double' Conigliaro, Simon 'why the ****
is it on top of the door' Ford, Stuart 'lap of glory' Bale, Steve 'I got something'
Olson, Stuart 'go on' Ekins, Sandrae Lawrence& Gary Sharpen 'oh go on then',
Spike 'you are so pooky' Merchant, Stuart 'my head hurts' Tilley, Thoma 'it's
cool' Girard, Tom 'the difference between' Whitehead, Wayne 'edamame'
Collins, Zoe 'I just blushed' Burgess.

To all the wonderful customers, employers and colleagues I have met on this
journey and the teams at 69 Colebrooke Row and the Zetter Townhouse for
putting up with some off-the-beaten track ideas... Anybody I have forgotten,
please accept my most sincere apologies...